INDIAN PRAIRIE PUBLIC LIBRARY DISTRICT

3 1946 00502 9738

W9-CJT-443

Understanding Green Building Guidelines

for Students and Young Professionals

Traci Rose Rider

Edited by Karen Levine

W. W. Norton & Company

New York • London

INDIAN PRAIRIE PUBLIC LIBRARY
401 Plainfield Rd.
Darien IL 60561

The following proprietary names are used in this book by permission of the owners: LEED®, Green Globes®, and The Natural Step® Austin Energy Green Building™; National Green Building Program™; NAHBGreen™ HealthyBuilt Homes©

Copyright © 2009 by Traci Rose Rider

All rights reserved
Printed in the United States of America
First Edition

For information about permission to reproduce selections from this book, write to Permissions, W. W. Norton & Company, Inc., 500 Fifth Avenue, New York, NY 10110

For information about special discounts for bulk purchases, please contact W. W. Norton Special Sales at specialsales@wwnorton.com or 800-233-4830

Manufacturing by Courier Westford
Book design by Jonathan D. Lippincott
Production manager: Leeann Graham

Library of Congress Cataloging-in-Publication Data

Rider, Traci Rose.
  Understanding green building guidelines : for students and young professionals / Traci Rose Rider ; edited by Karen Levine. — 1st ed.
    p. cm.
  Includes bibliographical references and index.
  ISBN 978-0-393-73263-4 (pbk.)
  1. Sustainable buildings—Design and construction. 2. Sustainable construction. 3. Sustainable architecture. I. Levine, Karen, 1950– II. Title.
  TH880.R53 2009
  720'.47—dc22
                                        2009017359

ISBN: 978-0-393-73263-4 (pbk.)

W. W. Norton & Company, Inc.
500 Fifth Avenue, New York, N.Y. 10110
www.wwnorton.com

W. W. Norton & Company Ltd.
Castle House, 75/76 Wells Street, London W1T 3QT

0 9 8 7 6 5 4 3 2 1

This book was printed on 80# Utopia Book, which is FSC-certified. The Forest Stewardship Council (FSC) sets forth principles, criteria, and standards for the wood fiber industry that span economic, social, and environmental concerns, meaning that the paper has passed through a complete "chain of custody" from an FSC-certified forest, to an FSC-certified paper manufacturer, to an FSC-certified merchant, and an FSC-certified printer. Each part of the chain has its own standards for compliance. The paper contains 10 percent post-consumer waste, and is elemental-chlorine free.

According to the paper mill's Web site (appletoncoated.com), use of this paper yields

Trees Saved: 3
Post-consumer recovered fiber (PCRF) displaces wood fiber with savings translated as trees. (The number of typical trees assumes a mix of hardwoods and softwoods 6-8" in diameter and 40' tall.)

Energy Saved: 2.2 million BTUs
PCRF content displaces energy used to process equivalent virgin fiber. (The average U.S. household uses 91 million BTUs of energy in a year.)

To my son, Beckett—may you love your future profession as much as I love mine, and to my husband, Dan—you are my balance.

Contents

Preface

Early in 2003, I was lucky enough to become involved with an incredible group of students and young professionals who were interested in and dedicated to the green building movement, but who lacked direction on how to get involved, where to go for information, and what resources to tap. Fascinated by anything having to do with green building strategies and issues of sustainability as they apply to the construction field, our small group formed the U.S. Green Building Council's (USGBC) Emerging Green Builders (EGB) Program. We discovered that there were many others out there, in schools and offices across the country, who were in the same position. In fact, the program exploded to 80+ local EGB programs in less than two years.

The green building movement has grown significantly over the past few years, accompanied by a corresponding appetite for information about every aspect of green building. Future leaders of the green building movement—students and young professionals—as well as traditional practitioners in the construction industry are getting actively involved and doing their best to wade through the rapidly changing strategies, organizations, standards, and players in the movement. The tidal wave of information has become a challenge to navigate and organize.

Many students are taking matters into their own hands, organizing campus groups to educate and advocate for green building. While courses on green building strategies and methods are being added to the academic curriculum, it is nearly impossible to cover every topic.

Young professionals are also being asked to jump head first into the process. Many have taken up the cause at their offices and are being asked to lead the way, developing in-house training and finding appropriate building systems. Naturally, many look first to the most popular or well-known source on the topic: for alternative energy, the search might lead to the popular world of photovoltaics; for energy efficiency, to Building Information (BIM) Modeling; and for greener materials, to local producers.

For a start in how to green a building, however, they may also turn to any number of green building guidelines and rating systems from one of the go-to organizations in the field or to one of the other valid and slightly different tactics for assessing buildings and construction, from the global scale down to the local. The primary purpose of this book is to provide interested students and professionals who are new to the world of green building with a roadmap through some of the guideline and rating system options available to them. While this book by no means covers all of the existing guidelines and rating systems, it does cover the major national providers of green building rating systems, as well as seven examples of approaches being used at the local level in cities across the United States. It is my hope that the book will provide enough information for readers to understand the goals, benefits, and limitations of each of these systems and make an educated selection that meets the goals, objectives, and circumstances of a project's developer and/or owner.

Because the whole sphere of green building is changing so rapidly (and, at times, rather dramatically), I encourage you to take these descriptions as simply a framework—a starting point—and with the understanding that the information is current only so long as no updated versions are released. Updates do come frequently, however, so please go to the source for details about any of these programs. Web sites and other resources are provided for that purpose.

The book also addresses the typical array of concerns that arise when talking about green building strategies. For example, nearly everyone is concerned with energy, materials, site, water, and indoor air quality. Because of the importance of these topics, they are covered in somewhat more detail in the chapter on LEED. In subsequent chapters about other rating systems, these topics are referred to in general terms unless there is something notable that needs to be pointed out, such as a difference in treatment, qualifications, standards, etc. My aim throughout is to provide a baseline of information and a means of comparison among the systems.

My goal for this book is that it succeeds in providing you with as much knowledge as I acquired while researching and writing it and that it gives you a solid overview of the many issues you need to understand and deal with when approaching the design and construction of a green building.

Acknowledgments

This project would not have happened without contributions from a wide variety of people, whether they are aware of their offerings or not. Much as it takes a village to raise a child, it took a village for me to be able to write this book. I wish to wholeheartedly thank the many people without whom the book would not have reached maturity.

First, there are those friends in the target audience who thoroughly reviewed different parts of the book and gave me great insights, suggestions for topics I overlooked, and further questions to address: Sharon Hout, whose valuable time could have been spent studying for the ARE; Katie Worley, for insight regarding scope and numerous helpful comments; and Jing Zhang, who looked with fresh eyes and helped me to remember that there is interest in green building outside of the design and construction fields.

Experts within the many organizations mentioned in this book generously took the time to review the sections pertinent to them, fact checking and clarifying along the way. Key among them were: Max Zahniser, Praxis Building Solutions, and a USGBC veteran; Katie Jensen, Austin Energy Green Building Multi-Family Program Coordinator, and a great resource, both personal and professional; Brad Wood, a good friend and green residence guideline expert extraordinaire, who could likely write his own book based on the residential market; Joshua Clements, Energy Independent Communities Assistant in the Wisconsin Office of Energy Independence, for his research and review; Dona Stankus and Jennifer Stutzman of the North Carolina Solar Center and HealthyBuilt Homes; Anthony Floyd, Scottsdale's Green Building Manager; Brenden McEneaney and Neal Shapiro, with the City of Santa Monica; Regina Hauser, of the Oregon Natural Step Network; Taryn Holowka, Jennifer Schill, Lauren Connelly, and Ashley Katz, of USGBC; Kevin Stover and Amanda Banker, of the Green Building Initiative; Joan Kelsch, Arlington County Environmental Planner; Valerie Garrett, of Portland's Green Building Hotline; Alisa Kane, the City of Portland's Green Building Coordinator; Cindy Bethell, of the Portland Development Commission; Emily English and Kevin Morrow, of the National Association of Home Builders; Robin Pharo, of Healthy Homes in Wisconsin; and Kathryn Schiedermayer, of Energy Center of Wisconsin.

I am grateful to my dissertation committee for allowing me to multitask: Dr. Wayne Place, North Carolina State University; Dr. Perver Baran, North Carolina State University; Professor Meredith Davis, North Carolina State University; and Dr. Madeleine Grumet, University of North Carolina at Chapel Hill.

My thanks also go to Nancy Green, at W. W. Norton, who believed in and supported this project from the start. Her enthusiasm and confidence helped make this, my first foray into the world of publishing, a really great experience. Then there's Karen Levine, my editor, who was an incredible guide with unflagging patience, profound insight, and fantastic questions. I was so lucky to have her on this project!

My cheering section and inspiration also includes Tripp Borstel, Amelia Doyle, Ryan Evans, Meghan Fay, Tim Hall, Jody Henry, Karol Kiser, Mary Ann Lazarus, Shelley McPhatter, Forrest Meggers, Ann Page, Maria Sutter, and Joe Snider. Each of you bolstered me throughout the process, often without knowing it. Gail Lindsay, I know your spirit is watching over the thousands you have inspired, and I am fortunate to be one of them. Kira Gould, your energy, enthusiasm, connections, and cheer never cease to amaze me. Thank you for thinking of me as often as you do! J. Matt Thomas, blessings not only for your priceless friendship but also for access to your research on local green building guidelines and policies. Susannah Tuttle—wonderful business partner—thank you for your encouragement, your research assistance, your help with the dirty work, and your help in keeping me on track, start to finish.

My family: my parents, Judy Lowrey and Tom Rose. You gave me the foundation—the belief in myself and the sheer determination to keep reaching. My brother, Jeff Lowrey, first for being my brother and second for serving our great country. My husband, Dan—your encouragement, support, patience, and humor mean the world to me. Thank you for making sure I was fed while I worked away all those evenings to finish. You challenge me like no one else, and I thank you for it. And, last but not least, I want to acknowledge the deadline of all deadlines, our firstborn child, Beckett Rider, due two weeks after the submission deadline for the manuscript. You were my greatest motivation for staying on schedule!

1: Navigating the Wild World of Green Building

An undeniable shift is occurring within our society. "Eco" has become a household word. Sustainable, earth-friendly, eco-friendly, organic, energy efficiency—all of these are such familiar terms that they pepper dinner table conversations, easily spanning the generations. In fact, it is almost hard *not* to think about the environment with the pervasiveness of it in all media. Journalists write and report about environmental issues in every print and digital format; special green episodes appear on television; cable channels have been created that are specifically geared toward the subject.

You can barely mention "green" or "sustainable" or other environmentally related terms without adding a qualifier or some level of specificity. Green what? Sustainable what? The options are too numerous to leave without clarification of the basic terms. There is, also, the larger question: What is sustainability? What does it mean to live in a sustainable manner? Sure, driving a hybrid is eco-friendly, but is it really sustainable? How about buying organic? Are you a better person for buying products that use compostable packaging? When talking about a sustainable way of life, there are a number of issues to look at, and rarely will you find just one "right" answer or direction. "Green" is not black and white, but rather a world composed of shades of gray in which each person has his or her own values, perspectives, and tolerances. What may be the best and greenest option for one may not be the best and greenest for all.

The same applies to green building. The realm of green building encompasses an incredible number of topics, issues, and compromises. As if there were not enough questions to deal with in the design and construction of a building *before* the emphasis on green building began, since its emergence the factors to be considered have multiplied in many diverse ways. Everything from species migration patterns to new carpet smells are now well within the realm of concern for green building practitioners.

That said, green building is but one of many important factors in achieving sustainability. Concerns about global warming, natural disasters, endangered species, carbon footprints, and resource depletion of fossil fuels and nonrenewable energy sources are highly complex subjects. It's difficult to determine exactly how big a contributing role building design and construction play in the larger picture, simply because everything is so intertwined. If the design and construction industries tried to look at all issues comprehensively for each project, the effort would be so overwhelming that nothing would get done. Designers would be spread so thin that they would not be able to focus on creating good, solid, valuable structures that are enjoyable, safe, and beautiful—the core of all that they are taught in design school. So where exactly does that line, that realm of influence, get drawn? What can we, as building design and construction industry professionals, address in our daily processes and products that will give us the best—and greenest—result without totally overwhelming us? Green building guidelines and rating systems provide us with a structure for answering that question.

Regardless of their individual approaches, rating systems are structured in a way that breaks down the considerations of green building design and construction into something manageable—that is, into criteria that an architect, designer, contractor, or anyone else in the construction industry can readily understand. The rating systems address all of the issues that design and construction industry professionals deal with on a daily basis, cross-referenced with the larger issues of sustainability. Green building encompasses not only a structure's energy use and material sources but also considerations of ecosystem preservation or restoration, regional watersheds, carbon footprints, even lifestyle. Given the interconnectedness of all of these, it is no surprise that these topics may enter the conversation during design and construction meetings. The intention behind the various guidelines is to give structure to the process, organizing the primary topics to be addressed and acknowledging any related topics that should also be considered. As with any product in a competitive marketplace, a number of different green building rating systems and guidelines have been created over the past decade or so and there may be more on the horizon. The variations among them are not unlike other choices in our lives—cars, jeans, residences, jobs. This book explores the array of options available and makes comparisons among the different alternatives so that construction professionals can consider their options objectively and pick the one that is right for their project and project team.

I've chosen to begin the exploration with the most recognizable rating system available in the United States: USGBC's LEED. Chapter 2 goes through the LEED system in a straightforward manner, looking at the structure of the system as well as the different categories and issues it addresses and how it does so. Because LEED is such a widely recognized system, I've used it as the standard against which to compare other systems in the subsequent chapters of the book. I do not mean to suggest by this choice that LEED is necessarily the best system available, only that it is the most well known. Other large-scale guidelines and rating systems are described in the subsequent chapters of the book. These systems include The Natural Step, Green Globes, and NAHBGreen developed by the National Association of Home Builders. Since Chapter 2 reviews both the topics covered by LEED as well as its system of credits, I have chosen not to burden readers with a review of similar credits for each of the other rating systems described unless there is a notable difference between a given system and the LEED system. The final chapter of the book explores how different localities have developed their own green building guidelines by taking a look at seven of the most respected and innovative local systems around the country.

Let's begin our survey of the current green building guidelines and rating systems by looking at the most prevalent: the U.S. Green Building Council's (USGBC) Leadership in Energy and Environmental Design (LEED®) Green Building Rating System. It is quite likely that you have already heard of USGBC and the LEED system, but just in case, I'll quickly review both the organization and its products.

The LEED system is a third-party green building certification system, currently the broadest, most widely known, and most frequently used certification system for green buildings in the United States. The system, however, doesn't stop at the individual building level; it has been expanded beyond that scale to encompass larger scopes, such as campuses and entire neighborhoods. I'll address the larger scale of application later. The LEED certification system was developed in 2000 by the volunteer, consensus-based committees of USGBC. The over-arching goal of USGBC is to drive market transformation within the building industry, essentially to make green building strategies the go-to system in everyday design and construction operations by awarding various levels of LEED certification to the highest performing projects.

LEED itself was not intended to be used as a standard on every building, but rather to highlight the leaders within the industry, encouraging others to jump on board with green building, and thereby create a paradigm shift. Instead of having to look specifically for materials with recycled content, for example, or for "green" alternatives to cabinetry to incorporate into a design, such a paradigm shift would mean that all available materials would be based on recycled content and there would no longer be an option for non-green cabinetry. In sum, the market itself—and all of the available options within it—would be inherently green.

By defining consistent criteria for green buildings, LEED guidelines provide a method of preventing *"greenwashing"* in the building industry because the system requires specified, verifiable outcomes as proof for certification. While not universal, USGBC's membership, product offerings, and local chapter programs continue to grow at an incredible rate, giving the organization an extraordinarily powerful position in leading the green building transformation.

> **Greenwashing:** *Merging two disparate ideas, "green" and "whitewashing," into one word, "greenwashing" refers to companies, products, or processes that are promoted as "green" but may not actually adhere to good environmental practices. Wikipedia and Terrachoice.com note that the term implies an intention to mislead consumers regarding the environmental practices of a company or the environmental benefits of a product or service. Think about it this way: if an organization puts up a green appearance but does not really value and manifest environmentally responsible practices, the organization is hoping consumers will see it through green-colored glasses. So when specifying materials or selecting products for a construction project, it's worth thinking about what facts exist to support a company's environmental claim before you set a spec or make a purchasing decision.*

2.1 A Snapshot of USGBC

To really understand what underpins a rating system as well as what that system is intended to achieve, we need solid information about the organization that has developed and is promoting the system. That is as true of green building guidelines as it would be of any system, product, or process, lest we risk putting our faith blindly in a faceless organization. So let's take a look inside USGBC's organizational structure and functions.

Nationally, USGBC is an organization of organizations. This may seem a little odd until you get your mind around it. Member companies, such as your firm or business, can join USGBC for an annual fee that is scaled based on the firm's gross annual revenue. USGBC's membership categories are wide-ranging: a broad spectrum of industry sectors and a diverse array of public and private sector organizations are represented within USGBC's membership ranks. More than likely, your organization will fit within one of USGBC's membership categories (as listed on the USGBC Web site):

- Contractors and Builders
- Corporate and Retail
- Educational Institutions (K–12, Universities and Research Institutions)
- Federal Government and Government-Owned Organizations
- Insurance Companies and Financial Institutions
- Nonprofit and Environmental Organizations
- Product Manufacturers, Building Controls, Service Contractors and Distributors

- Professional Firms (Architects, Accountants, Engineers, Planners, Press, etc.)
- Professional Societies and Trade Associations
- Real Estate and Real Estate Service Providers
- State and Local Governments
- Utilities and Energy Service Companies

When a firm becomes a USGBC member at the national level, that membership allows all of the member organization's employees to receive discounts on member services through USGBC's Web site. It also allows the member company's employees to serve on USGBC committees, including the LEED development committees and local chapter boards. Additional financial benefits include discounts to attend USGBC's national conference and local workshops and to purchase reference materials such as the LEED Reference Guides.

2.1.1 Organizational Structure at the National Level

While the structure of USGBC is organic and shifts to meet the needs of its membership, it has a basic organizational composition. A board of directors presides over the national organization. The individual members of the board are all volunteers. They come from across the United States and generally hold full-time jobs, typically in some aspect of the construction and related industries, and usually in a leadership capacity.

Board members are elected to the board annually by representatives of all USGBC member companies, one vote per member organization. This ensures that no member company (say one with 750 employees) carries more weight with respect to who gets elected to a national board seat than any other member company (such as one with only five employees). A certain number of spots are allocated to different constituencies to ensure representation of the various member organization categories (contractor, professional firm, product manufacturer, and so on). Because each of these different elements of the construction industry may have different perspectives and values, this breakdown aims to ensure that all voices within the green building discussion are represented. Board members typically serve a two-year term.

In addition to this all-volunteer governing body, USGBC has a full-time staff in the organization's headquarters in Washington, DC. The staff is led by a chief executive officer (CEO) who is based at USGBC's headquarters and who is the public face of the organization. Reporting to the CEO are a number of departments that work together to serve the mission of the organization and the needs of its member companies. As you might expect, the chief operating officer (COO) oversees all of the day-to-day activities and operations management of the association—the technology department, administrative support, finance, human resources, and overall governance within the organization.

USGBC's membership has grown rapidly since the early 2000s, in terms of both the number of member organizations and the number of local chapters. Accompanying that growth has been comparable growth in USGBC's educational initiatives, membership needs, and overall program development. At the same time, USGBC's staff has grown to keep pace with this increased demand for services and support, including: educational initiatives, program development, general guidance, and membership services. Individual departments that support these activities are Community; Advocacy and Public Policy; Education and Research; and LEED.

The Community department focuses on the development of the USGBC network, including all member firms and individuals. This includes supporting the entire local chapter program (which will be discussed briefly later) as well as the national membership program, including member services and benefits. The Community team also supports USGBC's student and young professional programs, the Emerging Green Builders (EGB) and USGBC Students. These structures, like the local chapter structure, are hosted both nationally and locally, and the Community department is all about keeping USGBC's membership happy, well informed, organized, and focused on the collective green building goal.

> **USGBC Local Chapters:** To find out more about your local chapter, visit USGBC's Web site at www.usgbc.org and click on the "Chapters" tab at the top.

> **USGBC's Emerging Green Builders (EGB) and USGBC Student Groups:** To see what other young professionals are doing in the field of green building and how you can get involved, visit the national EGB Web site. From the USGBC homepage at www.usgbc.org, click on "Chapters." There you'll find a link to the Emerging Green Builders homepage, as well as instructions on how to start a USGBC Student group. Local group activities differ depending on their local population. Many local EGB chapters host great events and design competitions and offer a variety of other ways, depending on your particular interests, for you to get involved.

The Advocacy and Public Policy department bridges the gap between initiatives for specific populations, such as local chapters and membership, and other more general educational elements in the form of industry outreach. This group includes marketing, communications, public policy, international affiliations, and various levels of advocacy (local, state, and federal).

The Education and Research department handles all of USGBC's educational programming, including conferences and events such as the annual Greenbuild International Conference and Expo, LEED educational programs (both online and instructor led), and the K–12 and Higher Education green

Greenbuild: *USGBC's annual Greenbuild International Conference and Expo has become the place to see and be seen in the green building industry. Held regularly each November in rotating cities, this conference officially started in 2003 in Pittsburgh, PA. By 2008, just five years later, the number of conference attendees had grown to 30,000+. You can keep up-to-date with the conference at www.greenbuildexpo.org.*

building curriculum, research, and education partnerships with member organizations.

The LEED department is USGBC's largest and most extensive—and with good reason. The LEED department and LEED committees are where all the rating system magic happens. The LEED department is in charge of all the prospective LEED registrations and certifications that are being submitted for review, as well as the support, technical development, and evolution of different versions of the rating systems. Under the LEED department's umbrella are Operations, National Accounts, and Technical Development.

LEED workshops may be one of the most familiar methods of education and outreach to the construction industry and the public. These workshops are typically hosted by local chapters and vary depending on what the hot topic is at the moment in that locale. A residential boom, calling for a review of LEED for Homes, or a number of companies relocating to downtown, might call for a LEED for Commercial Interiors overview. The workshop offerings can cover all of the LEED rating systems, carbon reduction methods, or even be profession specific, such as LEED for Contractors.

Another offering likely to rival the popularity of the LEED workshops is Greenbuild 365, launched at Greenbuild 2007. Greenbuild 365 is an online service that provides easy access to courses on green building right from your desktop. In addition, Greenbuild 365 showcases keynote speakers and sessions from the previous Greenbuild conferences, as well as other courses pertaining to green building available from other organizations. Much of the content is free.

2.1.2 Organizational Structure at the Local Level

Because sustainability happens most at the local level, local and regional USGBC chapters have sprung up around the country. These chapters are geared toward serving the green building needs of communities, governments, clients, and product manufacturing at the local level. Furthermore, while national membership is limited to companies and organizations, the local USGBC chapters cater heavily to individuals. The local chapters give individuals interested in green building the opportunity to take the initiative and get involved on their own, regardless of whether your employer is a member organization, though your company typically needs to be a national member company to occupy a local chapter board seat.

Each of the full USGBC chapters is established as a separate non profit organization with its own board of local professionals who lead their particular chapter. Many chapters mirror the structure of the national organization by having various committees such as finance, membership, education, outreach, and advocacy. Most chapters also have local committees of the Emerging Green Builders and USGBC Students to encourage student and young professional involvement. These smaller USGBC entities are perfect for local workshops, building tours, and networking.

2.2 LEED Lingo

If you want to sound knowledgeable about LEED, the first thing to be aware of is that the rating systems are called LEED, not LEEDs, Leed, or Leeds. Calling them LEEDs is a tip-off to those in the know that perhaps you aren't. Even when you're referring to multiple rating systems, you would say "LEED rating systems" and not "LEEDs." The only exception is when LEED's is used as a possessive—for example in a sentence that begins, "In LEED's Sustainable Sites category, you'll find . . ."

Second, when people take the test on the LEED rating system, they become LEED Accredited Professionals (LEED APs). They do not become LEED Certified. Only buildings become LEED Certified; people do not. Also, as far as that goes, building products cannot be LEED Certified, so watch out for that as you move through the design and construction process.

There is no LEED Certified steel, or carpet, or countertops. Remembering these points is fundamental to ensuring that you get off on the right foot in the world of USGBC and green building.

With the unveiling of LEED Version 3, a new set of LEED credentials were released. The first level of certification is Green Associate, indicating green building expertise for non-technical fields, such as legal and marketing. The LEED AP status continues to indicate advanced knowledge of green building, and will now also indicate the ability to specialize in a certain field, such as Operations and Maintenance, Interior Design and Construction, or Homes. Finally, the LEED Fellow designates outstanding individuals leading the green building movement. This level is still under development at the time of writing.

2.3 The Various LEED Programs

Most of the time when we think of LEED, we think of one building adhering to a set of parameters in order to achieve recognition for a certain standard of environmental responsibility. However, when you think about it, there are a number of different scenarios that may not fit into that big, overarching, general category. Back in the early 2000s, there was one single rating system called LEED. Since then, USGBC has launched a number of variations and adapted the original rating system structure accordingly to incorporate other possible construction options than simply a single building.

2.3.1 Application-Specific Versions of LEED

Because the possible types of buildings and projects in the construction industry vary greatly, USGBC has created several different versions of LEED to help guide green building methods across the board. These distinct interpretations address different types of construction, understanding that constructing a base building is very different from a speculative development project or those focusing on interiors. The different versions also look at various program types such as neighborhoods, schools, and retail spaces. These adaptations have been created to address technical and project scope differences not necessarily addressed by the original version of LEED, which focused on new construction and major renovations (listed first below). While things have changed slightly with the implementation of LEED 2009, launched in April 2009, which will be addressed later, the scope of LEED programs consists of:

- New Commercial Construction
- Commercial Interiors
- Existing Buildings: Operations & Maintenance
- Core & Shell
- Homes
- Neighborhood Development
- Portfolio Program
- LEED for Schools

- LEED for Retail (in pilot)
- LEED for Healthcare (in pilot)

Regardless of their individual focus, all LEED programs award certification, when merited, according to the following scale: Certified, Silver, Gold, and Platinum. In the original LEED system, LEED for New Construction Version 2.2, the point distribution historically looked like this:

- Certification: 26–32 points
- Silver: 33–38 points
- Gold: 39–51 points
- Platinum: 52–69 points

This point distribution changed with the rollout of LEED 2009 (described in section 2.5) and now uses 100 points. Be sure to refer to the Reference Guide applicable to your project to find out how you are being scored. Because the LEED for New Construction rating system is the one most widely used and with which the industry is most familiar, Version 2.2 of that system will be used throughout this chapter to provide examples of the system's Prerequisites and Credits in each category.

These individual LEED rating systems were not created in a vacuum. The LEED development committees are filled by volunteers who are experts in their particular disciplines (and supported by staff); these volunteer experts discuss various issues pertaining to the different LEED rating systems and implementation processes. Drawing their specialized knowledge, professional opinions, and research and testing, the committees continually incorporate changes into new versions of the guidelines. The rating systems are constantly under scrutiny from both staff and volunteers, as well as, of course, users, contributing to their ongoing value, applicability, and vigor as useful rating systems.

2.3.2 Getting Started with LEED

The intent of the LEED rating system is to break down green building into something manageable—to create criteria that an architect, designer, contractor, or anyone else in the building industry can understand and actually implement. What if your client (or boss or colleague) came to you one day and said, "Let's build a green building!" Where would you start? You might have to spend weeks on research to figure out what this "green building" concept is all about. Instead, LEED has taken that big, first step, developing a method that walks users of the rating system through a series of user-friendly categories and credits to create a green building.

For their part, USGBC's LEED rating systems have established primary categories that align with various areas of concentration for a design team. These categories are: Sustainable Sites, Water Efficiency, Energy & Atmosphere, Materials & Resources, Indoor Environmental Quality, and Innovation. Within these primary categories there are a number of pre-requisites and credits that can be targeted and potentially achieved during the design and construction processes.

The certification level that the team obtains depends thoroughly on dedication, client buy-in, teamwork, and coordination. Incorporating green building goals and strategies early in the design process, with the participation of the entire team, is also a key contributing factor in the level of success achieved.

2.4 Structure of the Rating Systems

Although about a dozen LEED rating systems have been established or are in development, many use similar components because they have all stemmed from LEED for New Construction in one way or another. As mentioned previously, the six categories most LEED rating systems have in common are: Sustainable Sites, Water Efficiency, Energy & Atmosphere, Materials & Resources, Indoor Environmental Quality, and Innovation.

The discussion below provides an overview of the Pre-requisites and Credits for each of these categories. For more detailed information, you will need to work with USGBC and refer to the various reference materials available. Also, USGBC holds workshops and webcasts on a variety of topics to help your team get moving and get your project done. For the moment, however, let's begin by reviewing the general layout of the rating system.

2.4.1 Rating System Prerequisites and Credits

The rating systems are built around *Prerequisites* and *Credits*. In each of the six categories, there are likely to be one or two issues noted as *Prerequisites*. The prerequisites must be met in order for the building to pursue LEED certification. If you don't hit all the prerequisites, you don't get certified. The remaining issues, delineated as *Credits*, are for the most part optional. Points are accrued for each of these credits and are combined to make up your potential final score—and your final rating. Keep in mind, though, that just because your team pursues a number of points does not mean you will achieve the rating that your team set as its goal. With that in mind, it is usually better to aim high.

To assist you in meeting your team's rating goals, the various LEED Reference Guides list a number of things that can help you figure out exactly what USGBC looks for with respect to each credit in the rating system. First, there is the rating system content itself, which outlines the "intent" of each credit (i.e., the type of impact USGBC is seeking), the "requirements" that need to be met in order to achieve the credit and receive the point (usually, there are different options available, providing varying degrees of beneficial impact, depending on your design's particular constraints, locale, strategies, and client preferences, goals, and objectives), and possible strategies and technologies that the design team could use to accomplish this intent and meet the requirements.

Following this introduction to the intent, credit, and associated points, USGBC runs through a list of additional details for each credit to guide you on your way to green building. These details include:

- Summary of Referenced Standards (in cases where an established standard is being used as a benchmark, such as ASHRAE 90.1-2004). ASHRAE refers to the American Society of Heating, Refrigerating and Air Conditioning Engineers, the professional organization for mechanical engineers.
- Approach to Implementation (other constraints and departments you may want to consider, such as legal or technical issues)
- Calculations (if needed for that particular credit)
- Exemplary Performance (outlining the possibility of exceeding the guideline standards if applicable)
- Submittal Documentation (what exactly you need to provide for USGBC to understand and believe what you are talking about)
- Considerations (additional issues that the design team may need to think about in the design and planning phases, such as environmental, social, community, and economic issues or synergies within the design)
- Resources (for example, organizations, Web sites,

journals, and books that can be used as the design team attempts to seamlessly integrate the credit)

- Definitions (anything in the previous sections that may be confusing or vague to anyone, just to make sure there is no confusion).

An incredible amount of information is listed in the LEED Reference Guides. Given the space limitations of the printed guides, USGBC provides additional information on its Web site as a centralized resource for both national members and those on LEED project teams. This information includes Reference Guide errata, as well as the following.

2.4.2 Credit Interpretation Rulings

Even after looking at all the references and guidelines to make sure each credit is understood, the team, as it moves forward, may still have some uncertainty around the gray areas that can occur in construction or about whether what the team is doing is exactly what USGBC requires to receive credit for a certain point. It's simply not possible when developing a rating system to anticipate every potential issue or circumstance that LEED project teams may face.

To address these unforeseen issues—and to clarify as needed over the course of a project—LEED project teams can request Credit Interpretation Rulings (CIRs) during the design and submission process, as well as the opportunity to review rulings that previous projects have received. The CIR is just what it sounds like: a team can ask for an interpretation of a certain credit and how that credit may specifically apply to the team's project.

USGBC staff members and the relevant volunteer Technical Advisory Group (TAG) provide interpretations of the rules governing the credits and guidance if the team is feeling uncertain about a particular issue. The TAGs are advisory groups composed of professionals and experts from a specific field who have the expertise to review and rule on a team's questions or matters of interpretation. For example, in a larger development where only one building is being considered for certification, there may be a question as to how a stormwater detention pond may be divided and applied to the project. In another instance, there may be a question about the number of bike racks needed for a project servicing the elderly or the disabled. Arguably, these populations would not be able to use bikes as frequently as the standard building population. Again, once a project has been registered, the team can also view rulings that previous projects received on topics relevant to the project at hand. It is very useful to review these precedents thoroughly because there is a good chance that another team has already faced a similar situation and question.

2.5 LEED 2009

With the continual evolution of the market, USGBC, and the rating systems themselves, there is always a new version.

LEED 2009, or LEED v.3, is the next step. One impetus for this new version is to bring LEED to a point of continuous improvement and, in the process, to develop a Predictable Development Cycle that will allow the market to understand both when changes will take place and the expected future development of the tool.

Earlier, I noted how LEED grew from one system into a variety of rating systems based on project type. LEED 2009 returns to the concept of one set of LEED criteria, forming a foundation or "common denominator." LEED 2009 is predicated on there being an inherent logic built into the registration and rating system selection process. The LEED credits, as well as the prerequisites, have gone through a "harmonization" process: they have been unified to provide a common baseline for all LEED rating systems. All common credits have been extracted from the different rating systems and placed onto what is being called a "bookshelf." Each "book" represents one credit and contains different versions of the credit, as they pertain to different rating systems. For example, there may be one "book" for Site Selection. It outlines the different nuances based on whether the project is qualified as a New Construction project, a Commercial Interiors project, and so forth. The bookshelf will get filled out over time, pulling experience, questions, and clarifications from actual projects as they are completed. Rating systems for each building type and each location will be created; similarities will be captured in the core section of credits. This new structure requires a new reference guide, although the older ones can still be helpful for insights, precedents, and ideas.

LEED 2009 also redefines the point thresholds necessary for certification. A newly allocated 100 points will be possible under LEED 2009. Be sure to check the new Reference Guide and USGBC's Web site regarding this and other details about the specific point counts in LEED 2009. An additional six points will be available within the Innovation in Design category, and another four in a new Regional Priority category. This will be discussed below with respect to regional issues. A Water Efficiency prerequisite has been introduced in the new LEED 2009 system. As a result, the certification threshold has changed from a minimum of twenty-six points as in Version 2.2 to the following:

- Certification: 40–49 points
- Silver: 50–59 points
- Gold: 60–79 points
- Platinum: 80+ points

Another new factor in LEED 2009 is LEED weighting, which allows for a common denominator within topic areas, but also enables shifting and emphasis for greater positive impact on energy efficiency amd emission reduction. The new rating system uses weighting categories taken from the EPA's existing TRACI tool—that is, the Tool for the Reduction and Assessment of Chemical and Other Environmental Impacts (www.epa.gov/nrmrl/std/sab/traci/)—and of no relation to the author of this book. The weighting categories include: Climate Change; Resource Depletion; Human Health Criteria; Water Intake; Human Health (cancerous); Ecotoxicity; Eutrophication; Habitat Alteration; Human Health (non-cancerous); Smog Formation; Acidification; Indoor Air Quality; and Ozone Depletion. The categories have been divided into meta-categories of "direct human benefit" and "direct environmental benefit." This approach allows the rating systems to begin addressing issues such as social equity and to reward addressing priority issues.

Also included in the LEED weighting process are elements drawn from the U.S. Department of Commerce's Building for Environmental and Economic Sustainability (BEES) weighting system. Based on USGBC's values, it prioritized the various elements it drew from the TRACI and BEES weighting systems when incorporating them into the LEED 2009 credits and rating system.

USGBC also relied on scientific experts and research to help make informed decisions determining the most important environmental issues for the construction industry to address. In the process, USGBC gathered important local community input regarding aspects of the LEED system that could be improved.

LEED 2009 assumes that the past standard building process and product no longer apply and establishes the base case of a building as an average LEED building. In other words, the

Building for Environmental and Economic Sustainability (BEES): This software, developed by the U.S. Department of Commerce's National Institute of Standards and Technology (NIST), enables project teams to better select cost-effective, environmentally preferable building products. BEES was created through consensus standards, and values transparency, practicality, and flexibility. The tool adheres to the ISO 14040 life cycle approach to evaluating materials, including raw material harvesting, manufacture, transportation, installation, use, and end-of-life recycling and waste management. Cost assessment is looked at by way of up-front costs, anticipated replacement, operation, standard maintenance and repair, and end-of-life disposal. Download BEES free from www.bfrl. nist.gov/oae/software/bees/.

previous base case did not take the environment into account in any spectacular way. However, as the green building conversation progresses, this is no longer the case; USGBC now assumes that each building is starting to address the environment, at least a little.

The new version of LEED allows for the selection of differing degrees of various impacts—low, medium, or high—illustrating where most of the carbon emissions are coming from and emphasizing the key area of focus for the design team.

With this, the team will see more points in Transportation and Energy, and an associated change to EA (Energy and Atmosphere) Prerequisite 1 and the fundamental commissioning required. You can find the details in the new Reference Guide and literature on LEED 2009.

Another new element in LEED 2009 is the inclusion of regional concerns in the rating system. Simply put, this recognizes that individual issues have different levels of importance in different areas of the country, and LEED 2009 provides the ability to break down issues regionally or locally. Local USGBC chapters and regions were asked to identify six points that were important to their specific area. Using the input of local experts across the various fields involved with green building and sustainability, certain issues were identified as being particularly important in their specific region. LEED 2009 enables a project to garner more points based on the way it addresses the key issues in its particular locale. Instead of only one point for a particular credit in a given region, two points may be awardable. For example, in a region that is highly concerned about water use, such as the Southwest, extra credits can be achieved in the water categories, in contrast with other areas of the country where water usage is not as critical an issue, such as the Northwest. LEED 2009 also provides the opportunity for a project to earn six bonus points in the Innovation in Design category, and four of these bonus points can be earned as Regional Bonus Credits.

2.6 Registration and Submission Process

USGBC has a preferred process for registering and submitting a building for LEED certification. The first step is to register your project with USGBC. This step alerts USGBC that you are out there, with a real project, and interested in achieving some level of LEED certification. Your team should do this as early in the design process as feasible. Through this registration process, your team will receive additional access to tools, resources, and information from USGBC that will help you along the way, namely CIRs and also LEED-Online and its support systems (more below about LEED-Online).

Your team can register a project online through the USGBC Web site, www.usgbc.org, or by printing out the registration form from the Web site and mailing it (though this option may disappear in an increasingly digital world). The current registration form asks basic questions, such as the LEED rating system you are using; general project information (including the name of the project, confidentiality status, etc.); the project contact information (better for your team if that person is a LEED AP); project owner information (name, organization, email); and additional project details. These details are all easy to provide, even at the initial stages of design; they include the type of owner (government, non profit, etc.), site conditions, gross square footage, project budget, and the phase the project is in at the time the registration is submitted. Note, however, that the particular questions have shifted slightly with the rollout of LEED 2009.

There are fees associated with the project registration process. For corporate/national member companies registering a project in which they are involved, the registration fee (as of early 2009) is $450. If no one on the team is a corporate member, or someone else registers the project, the registration fee is $600.

Project registration simply gets your project into the system, opening the lines of communication with USGBC. Additional fees are incurred for the certification review; those will be addressed later in this chapter. Once the project gets registered, your team will be well on its way.

It's worth mentioning, particularly if you've been involved in the LEED certification process in the past, that LEED has streamlined its certification process significantly over the last few years. Originally, the process started with each project team having to submit a great deal of printed documentation. There was a spreadsheet to help manage the process. It had a few dozen tabs to record information! This was not only burdensome to the individuals on the project team who had to collect that information, but equally (if not more) burdensome for those at USGBC trying to manage multiple projects as they came in for review. Not only did USGBC need to have these files on record, they then also needed to send a copy (one of the two required) of the information to the third-party verification teams, making the process long and paper-intensive.

To address this, USGBC streamlined its registration process, which can now be completed online through LEED-Online. LEED-Online is the Web-based system by which project teams document compliance with all the prerequisites and pursued credits. It completely replaces the volumes of hard-copy documentation previously required.

Project administrators (LEED-Online's term for project team leaders relative to LEED certification) can work on credit documentation, assign credits to other team members to document, and ultimately submit the project for certification. From within this program, all the required LEED-Online forms can be accessed and managed, one for each prerequisite and credit. These online forms are usually referred to as "submittal templates" or "credit templates."

The credit templates help the team with project calculations and organization, reducing the headaches all around. Project team members can fill out the forms and pass them on within the team as necessary for further information. As the forms are filled out, supporting documents can also be uploaded to LEED-Online alongside the forms, as appropriate. This system allows the project administrators to view the documentation from their entire team online to ensure that it is complete and accurate prior to submission.

When everything is filled out and uploaded, the project is ready to be submitted for certification review. Once the project team has submitted all of its documentation, LEED-Online allows USGBC staff and third-party verification consultants access to the information online, eliminating the need and associated cost of hard-copy distribution. Project administrators can later view online USGBC's review rulings and comments, taking note of any additional issues that need to be addressed.

Teams now also can submit a project in two separate phases—design and construction—as opposed to submitting all the documentation at once at the end of construction and after occupancy. In this two-phased submission, design credits are usually submitted after construction documents are issued, when the associated documentation is recorded and decisions have been made. As the design submittal is reviewed, comments are provided to the design team, allowing slight alterations or clarifications if necessary before the final submission. This initial review allows project teams the opportunity to assess the likelihood of credit achievement; however, it also requires follow-through to ensure that the design is executed in the construction phase according to the design specifications. This gives the project team a clear understanding of what credits will be awarded if the project is built as designed. At the completion of construction, the project team submits all attempted credits for review. If the project team elected to have a design phase review and any of the design phase anticipated credits subsequently changed, additional documentation must be submitted to substantiate continued compliance with credit requirements.

By allowing this breakout of submission, LEED helps manage the volume of information that the project manager needs to keep organized, but more importantly addresses design-team-related issues while the design team is still engaged. Many building projects can take more than a year to construct, and if the design team is receiving comments on its LEED documentation that long after design, it can be very challenging to reengage in the project team efficiently and productively.

As your team begins the submission review process, you must go through a brief exercise by which your certification fee is determined. The fee covers the review process and certification itself. The fee varies depending on whether you have member or non-member status and also by building size and the review phase for which you are submitting: design review, construction review following a design review, or combined review with both phases reviewed at once. For example, for a combined (full) review of buildings under 50,000 square feet, the fee as of April 2009 was a fixed rate of $1,750 for members and $2,250 for non-members. Using this as an example, you can see how being a USGBC member would be beneficial, particularly if multiple buildings are pursuing LEED certification. You'll find the current fees posted on the USGBC Web site.

Sometimes the anticipated fees alone are enough to make a client or company balk at pursuing LEED certification, though there is little substance to this claim once all the calculations are made; more about that later. For now, let's take a closer look at the six primary categories (mentioned briefly in section 2.4: Structure of the Rating Systems) for which your project can earn LEED credits. The following is based on LEED Version 2.2, so keep in mind that the point allotment discussed has changed with LEED 2009.

2.7 Sustainable Sites

This category looks primarily at what happens outside the structure of the building and how unintended environmental impacts will be mediated. A number of the credits are well within the scope of the design team, but often are simply not thought through carefully enough. The credits in the Sustainable Sites category are:

- Prerequisite 1 Construction Activity Pollution Prevention
- Credit 1 Site Selection
- Credit 2 Development Density & Community Connectivity
- Credit 3 Brownfield Redevelopment
- Credit 4.1 Alternative Transportation (Public Transportation Access)
- Credit 4.2 Alternative Transportation (Bicycle Storage & Changing Rooms)
- Credit 4.3 Alternative Transportation (Low-Emitting & Fuel-Efficient Vehicles)
- Credit 4.4 Alternative Transportation (Parking Capacity)
- Credit 5.1 Site Development (Protect or Restore Habitat)
- Credit 5.2 Site Development (Maximize Open Space)
- Credit 6.1 Stormwater Design (Quantity Control)
- Credit 6.2 Stormwater Design (Quality Control)
- Credit 7.1 Heat Island Effect (Non-Roof)
- Credit 7.2 Heat Island Effect (Roof)
- Credit 8 Light Pollution Reduction

The prerequisite for this category, Construction Activity Pollution Prevention, asks the team to think specifically about the way in which the building will be constructed on the site. When we talk about process, we are not talking about design details per se, but rather the process the contractors will use when preparing the site, getting set up, and bringing in materials throughout construction—and how this preparation process will affect the greater ecosystems. This prerequisite looks at such aspects as the control of soil erosion during construction and how much of the site is disturbed, as well as dust generation and the contribution of additional sediment into the local waterways. Site selection, target density, and ecosystem disturbance are three important overarching issues in meeting this prerequisite. Each is discussed in turn below.

2.7.1 Site Selection-Related Credits

The overall issue of site selection is largely addressed by Credits 1 and 3:

- Credit 1 Site Selection
- Credit 3 Brownfield Redevelopment

Site selection credits look at what type of site has been chosen for the program. Is it a virgin site—one that has never been disturbed? Or is it a previously developed site, which may lessen the impact on natural systems? Is the program going into an existing building, creating even less of a burden on existing natural systems? While a project is often brought to the architect with a site already selected, the Site Selection credit gives an incentive to owners, developers, and designers to think carefully about what type of site they are selecting and what impacts their project will have on the environment.

Another favored option is to select a brownfield site—that is, a site that was developed previously and is now environmentally contaminated. Owners tend to shy away from these types of sites because of the real or perceived threat of the contaminants, or the real or perceived cost of cleaning the site to render it healthy and usable. Examples may be an old industrial site, an old gas station, or a factory of some kind—even a project that is filled with asbestos. By selecting a brownfield site for your project, you not only leave undeveloped land untouched, you also benefit the greater environment by cleaning up someone's past pollution. There are companies that purchase brownfield sites, clean them up, and sell them for redevelopment. One might be just right for your project!

2.7.2 Target Density-Related Credits

The Sustainable Sites section also tries to encourage the development of close communities by means of these credits:

- Credit 2   Development Density & Community Connectivity
- Credit 4.1 Alternative Transportation (Public Transportation Access)
- Credit 4.2 Alternative Transportation (Bicycle Storage & Changing Rooms)
- Credit 4.3 Alternative Transportation (Low-Emitting & Fuel Efficient Vehicles)
- Credit 4.4 Alternative Transportation (Parking Capacity)

"Close" refers to communities and neighborhoods that are more walkable, well integrated, and diverse. For example, rather than focusing on sites in a rural or more suburban locations, or even in office parks, these five credits encourage development in higher density areas where residents and employees can find services and entertainment in a smaller, more environmentally friendly radius. Depending on where they live, employees may be able to walk to work, and it is also more likely they will be able to walk to lunch or run errands without spending hours in the car expanding their carbon footprint.

In areas of greater density, residents are encouraged to use public and alternative transportation. Mass transit, carpooling, and even biking to work become more viable when the radius encompassing work, residential, and support services, such as the grocery, church, library, and post office, is reduced. To measure these criteria, different radii are established to define desirable target densities for residential and mixed-use neighborhoods and also what is walkable; these established distances are referenced in Credit 2.

Many individuals, however, will still want to drive to work and to run errands. The LEED credits promote sustainable choices indirectly by encouraging less overall parking and the provision of preferred parking spaces for those who carpool or who drive alternatively fueled vehicles.

2.7.3 Ecosystem Disturbance-Related Credits

Other credits in the Sustainable Sites grouping speak directly to the impact on local ecosystems by understanding that, as we build, we will obviously be disturbing various levels of ecosystem life. These credits include:

- Credit 5.1 Site Development (Protect or Restore Habitat)
- Credit 5.2 Site Development (Maximize Open Space)
- Credit 6.1 Stormwater Design (Quantity Control)
- Credit 6.2 Stormwater Design (Quality Control)
- Credit 7.1 Heat Island Effect (Non-Roof)
- Credit 7.2 Heat Island Effect (Roof)
- Credit 8 Light Pollution Reduction

Often, when a site is cleared (unarguably necessary to some extent for construction), the organisms and ecosystems that are being destroyed or displaced are simply seen as a tradeoff for what is to come. The credits address ecosystem-centered goals in several important ways by:

- Encouraging the preservation of some green space on the site when construction is complete;
- Ensuring that any plantings in the new landscape are native, thereby fostering the development of local ecosystems and reducing the maintenance necessary for upkeep;
- Reducing stormwater runoff quantity and managing stormwater quality so that contaminants from the new site (car oil, pesticides, etc.) and the amount of water not absorbed into the site will not overload the sewers and affect communities downstream;

- Managing the development of heat islands, which are usually impacted by surfaces (such as blacktop) that absorb heat and release it, raising the immediate temperature of the air around the site, which, in turn, can dramatically affect smaller, native ecosystems;
- Controlling light pollution—or excess or obtrusive light—that can reduce energy waste and ecosystem disruption and also improve human health and psychology.

Each of these represents ways in which site design choices can impact ecosystems if left unconsidered.

2.7.4 Calculations and Documentation

Without going into the technicalities of what is required as proof, you should be aware that your design team may need to prepare various calculations in order to receive some of the Sustainable Site credits. The calculations may include distance diagrams, sketches, or plans, such as those needed as proof to receive the credit for alternative transportation access within one-quarter mile of two public transportation stops.

2.8 Water Efficiency

Even before the southeast United States suffered an unprecedented drought in 2007–2008, water was a major concern in the country and beyond, in terms of both quality and quantity, depending on the location. While many of us were simply on serious water restrictions, many people had no access at all to drinking water. Water Efficiency, however, deals primarily with water quantity. USGBC states that the annual water deficit in the United States is estimated at approximately 3,700 billion gallons. That's a lot of water our country needs to be saving! The LEED Water Efficiency category of credits deals with the reduction of potable (drinking grade) and non-potable water usage in the designs of buildings and their associated sites. While currently this is the smallest LEED category with no prerequisites (prior to LEED 2009) and just five possible points through three credits, it remains of great importance. The credits that apply to the conservation of water are:

- Credit 1.1 & 1.2   Water-efficient landscaping: reduce by 50% or use no potable water or irrigation
- Credit 2   Innovative wastewater technologies
- Credit 3.1 & 3.2   Water use reduction: reduce by 20% or 30%

All of these credits have to do with water either coming into or leaving the building or site. Distinct from the stormwater management credits that fall within the Sustainable Sites category, Water Efficiency credits address the water that the design team actively brings into the scope of the project and uses in some fashion, be it in water fountains, toilets, lavatories, and other fixtures, or outside in irrigation.

2.8.1 Outdoor Water Use: Water-Efficient Landscaping

One of the key questions here is what uses a project actually does need to pull water for, and what quality of water is required for those uses. For example, is drinking grade water really *needed* to water the plants on the intricately crafted flower beds adorning our designs? Do we *need* to plant species in our landscape that are non-native to the region and therefore require more maintenance and support, including water, fertilizer, labor, and energy? This credit encourages design teams to look at design decisions not only from the desired aesthetics for the designed landscapes but also at the water consumption that will be required to support them.

While on the topic of water consumption in a designed landscape, one might ask if it is necessary to "design" irrigation systems that not only dutifully provide water to the plants that have been chosen for the landscape but also frequently water the paving as well. We have all seen huge rooster tails of water spraying narrow plantings while simultaneously (and unnecessarily) watering many times that area of pavement. These are the types of questions posed by the Water Efficiency credits that need to be considered during design.

Ideally, it would be best to create landscapes that do not require additional water above and beyond what is provided naturally by rainfall in the region. A vast amount of literature exists, both printed and online, that addresses varieties of native plantings for nearly every region around the world, and especially in the United States. The constructed, desired American lush lawn was not always the rage, and although there can be quite a discussion about the aesthetics and inheritance of traditional manicured gardens received from Europe, there is also decent support for the more natural-looking landscapes of other regions that do not require the same degree of management or water and energy resources. Regardless of which side your individual aesthetic tastes run to, as environmentally conscious individuals we should all subscribe to the idea that scarce water is better used for some purpose other than watering the snapdragons out front, and choose water uses consciously and conscientiously, giving preference to native species.

We would be remiss not to consider the alternative watering methods that LEED suggests, such as harvesting rainwater or recycled graywater, or wastewater created from processes in the building such as that from laundry and sinks, for use in the landscape. Although these methods do not specifically provide water naturally to the area without human intervention, they do not pull groundwater from the sorely depleted aquifers that are more and more prevalent in certain areas of the globe. The argument could be made that this collected and reclaimed water could be used elsewhere in the design, after the necessary treatments, and that is true to some extent, in some places. Some cities and counties have been persuaded to allow rainwater to be piped in to flush toilets, but with a little plaque stating that "toilet water is not for drinking." (Just in case we needed reminding.) However, unless you work in one of the more progressive places around the map, building codes often make it fairly difficult to use reclaimed wastewater or even collected rainwater for much more than outdoor irrigation.

2.8.2 Indoor Water Use

A vast amount of water comes into commercial buildings and much of it is wasted. How much unnecessary or unused water is sent down toilets and into drains every day in corporate America? The number would probably make our heads spin.

With respect to indoor water use, the credits focus primarily on lightening the load on aquifers and other water supplies, making it possible to start chipping away at the enormous deficit that has been created over the last seventy years or so. For example, by applying water efficiency strategies, water use in commercial buildings can be reduced by 30 percent or more, primarily through the use of sensors, low-flow fixtures, aerators on faucets, or non-water fixtures such as waterless urinals and composting toilets.

2.9 Energy and Atmosphere

One of the biggest and most daunting sections of LEED for beginners is the Energy and Atmosphere section, known in the LEED credit world simply as EA. These credits deal with the overarching issues of design and construction, which many individuals outside of the industry understand in principle and hear about on a daily basis. The topics in the EA category pertain to energy use and performance, emissions and greenhouse gasses, and energy generation. The credits in this section are as follows:

- Prerequisite 1 Fundamental Commissioning of the Building Energy Systems
- Prerequisite 2 Minimum Energy Performance
- Prerequisite 3 Fundamental Refrigeration Management
- Credit 1 Optimize Energy Performance
- Credit 2 On-Site Renewable Energy
- Credit 3 Enhanced Commissioning
- Credit 4 Enhanced Refrigeration Management
- Credit 5 Measurement and Verification
- Credit 6 Green Power

2.9.1 Commissioning and Measurement

A number of prerequisites are required for compliance in this category. First, the building has to be commissioned at a basic level.

Commissioning is not a word you hear a lot until you get into the land of green building and energy efficiency. Basically, it means that someone is checking that the systems in the building—such as HVAC, water, and lighting—were installed the way in which they were designed, have been calibrated to the specific needs of the design, and perform as they were designed to perform.

From the energy perspective, this primarily requires an energy model of the building that can be compared to established baseline numbers for a typical building of that type in your region. If the energy model for the designed building showed a 55 percent reduction in energy usage, the building systems would need to be installed and performing at the rate for which they were designed. It is no good at all if you design the building systems for one level, and they are installed to perform in a totally different fashion. Verification that all systems—HVAC, refrigeration, lighting, hot water, and any renewable energy generated on-site—are actually performing to the design specifications is required to meet this prerequisite. Control networks—or the brains of the different systems telling each how to operate, and usually tucked away in the mechanical room—for all of these systems need to be verified and assessed as well.

Different levels of commissioning exist and these are associated with a different number of credit points. The first level is a prerequisite and requires a basic level of commissioning for all systems; the additional LEED credit for "additional commissioning" as seen in EA Credit 3 incorporates other user-friendly elements, such as training for the personnel who run the systems, the creation of a systems manual for systems that have been commissioned, and periodic reviews of the construction documents during the design phases. There is also a follow-up visitation after the building has opened as part of additional commissioning to make sure system settings have not been shifted and the systems are still running as intended. This last step helps to ensure that the staff understands how to run and maintain the systems and that the systems are continuing to produce the desired effect and savings.

Since it is an exercise in verification, this additional commissioning work must be done by an outside source, which means the commissioning agent cannot be a member of the design team. Someone independent of the project, usually from another engineering firm, needs to come in to verify the design and the systems. Similar to the external verification that the LEED process provides, having an external source validate the intent and measurements of the building's energy systems strengthens the commissioning process. Numerous commissioning and verification firms are available to provide this service. A simple online search or a call to your local USGBC chapter should produce the necessary leads.

2.9.2 Credit for Verification

In addition to commissioning, there is a potential credit for verification that all the systems are continuing to work as planned over a specified period of time. This point can be found in EA Credit 5. The goal here is to make sure that the building *continues* to run as designed, preferably over the long haul. Ideally, this monitoring by the owners and/or occupants quickly identifies any shift in the primary energy systems and verifies the associated savings (or loss if something goes awry). For instance, there are often overrides on lighting sensors and thermostat settings, which can be changed if occupants feel it is necessary. Settings in the main HVAC and lighting systems can also be altered, which would obviously shift the performance of these systems and, in turn, alter the designed energy and monetary savings.

The potential monitoring and verifying of system function not only contributes to the continuous accountability of the systems and associated energy performance but also can serve as a highly valuable educational tool. A number of schools have been designed and built with the intention of serving as more than simply a facility students are taught in, but rather as one in which the building actively teaches students about issues such as energy usage and savings. Sidwell Friends Middle School in Washington, DC, designed by Kieran Timberlake Associates, is one example. The school received a LEED for New Construction Platinum rating with 57 points. Its students are encouraged to engage with the monitoring systems around the building to understand their use of resources and their contribution to the state of the environment.

IslandWood, an environmental center housed on Bainbridge Island, Washington, is another example of using monitoring systems to educate a facility's users. Mithun, a Seattle-based architectural firm, helped the organization achieve LEED Gold in the project. The firm invented a variety of ways for the fifth- and sixth-grade students who regularly visit the site to engage with the building. Some of the simpler strategies include operable windows and skylights and compostable toilets. While there are a number of sophisticated measurement tactics that relate to the actual active HVAC systems, there are also simpler versions at work to help students become cognizant of energy consumption within the building. Sun angles are recorded on the walls in the corridors with masking tape to visually demonstrate the difference between the winter and summer sun angles. A steel weight named Wade makes certain that everyone knows how much food is wasted at each meal. While these are not the technical measurement strategies noted in the LEED guidelines, they are nonetheless important in the educational aspects designed into the building. Each of the strategies helps students understand their own behaviors and those of their classmates in relationship to the built and natural environment.

While undoubtedly it is easiest to incorporate educational factors into schools and environmental centers because people are actually there to learn, do not overlook the opportunities that abound in any other building type. One of the primary ways to get people—adults—excited and engaged in the dialogue surrounding green building is to create an enjoyable and dynamic building that they actually want to enter into a relationship with. You may think that having a relationship with a building sounds silly, but it can be very powerful. You need think no further than your feelings about your childhood home (positive or negative) to know that a relationship with a building just needs an opportunity to develop.

2.9.3 Optimizing Energy Performance

Energy performance is another substantial topic in this category. The prerequisite for maximizing energy performance essentially asks that all buildings meet the ASHRAE Standard 90.1/2004 (90.1/2007 for LEED 2009). In many places, this is similar to what is required by code. The ASHRAE standard addresses the building envelope, HVAC requirements, water heaters, power requirements, lighting requirements, and additional equipment that may be in the building.

EA Credit 1 takes the energy performance of the building further than simply being "energy efficient." It puts specific values on levels of conservation through the awarding of LEED points. Depending on the percentage of energy actually saved in the design compared to the established baseline for that building type in that region, there is a sliding scale for the points that can be achieved for energy efficiency. For example, if a building is 10.5 percent more efficient than the minimum established in the prerequisite, the building gets one point. If it is 14 percent

> **Architecture 2030 Challenge & LEED:** *A number of organizations, including the American Institute of Architects (AIA), have adopted the 2030 Challenge. The Challenge states that all new construction should immediately be achieving 50% energy level reductions. Since EA Credit 1 gives a building with 42% energy reduction all ten possible points for the credit, a project will be well on its way should you decide to embrace the 2030 Challenge for it.*

more efficient, it gets two points, and so on up to being 42 percent more efficient, which nets the project team ten points. As of June 26, 2007, a project must achieve at least two points in this category to receive any level of LEED certification; in LEED 2009 this credit potential has increased to nineteen ponts. This requirement is a reflection on a number of recent waves within the building industry, including the Architecture 2030 Challenge, which advocates that all new construction be carbon neutral by the year 2030.* General energy concerns within the greater population are also a cause for this change. Popular and municipal forces supporting green building are gaining momentum. USGBC and LEED reflect these rapid changes in the market, incorporating this new requirement into the third edition of LEED for New Construction 2.2, which was issued in 2007.

*www.architecture2030.org

Although EA Credit 1, Optimize Energy Performance, hinges primarily on the execution of whole building energy models to understand, incorporate, and calculate the projected energy use of the design, there are other possibilities for achieving these credits, among them keeping the building office-use only and under 20,000 square feet. As discussed previously, there are now opportunities in the LEED program to submit much of the required documentation before construction, in phases, which helps lighten the burden for both the LEED review staff at USGBC headquarters and your design team. This approach also gets your team feedback early on some of the credits including energy modeling, allowing you to make small shifts in strategy if appropriate and feasible. But how will you know if the design intent has been met, you might ask? Through the commissioning components, of course.

It is imperative that all team members, including the MEP engineers, be involved in achieving EA Credit 1. It's beyond the scope of this book to go into all the details of required baseline parameters, the numerous calculations that need to be made to achieve these credits, or the tables of included Performance Rating Method Compliance Reports. Suffice to say here, if you are going to pursue a LEED certification for your building, you are going to need the applicable LEED Reference Guide. That publication explains the requirements (and more) in great detail. Keep in mind that your engineers are as integral a part of your design team as are all the other members. The energy model your engineers develop can help influence the choice of exterior skin, the amount of insulation or type of glass that will achieve the best results for the project, the necessary wall thickness, the appropriate materials, and more. The sooner you get everyone on board and on the same page, the more smoothly the process is likely to go.

2.9.4 Generating On-site Renewable Energy

The Energy and Atmosphere category of the LEED system looks beyond how much energy your building uses to examine the source of your energy. Up to three credits have been available for the generation and use of onsite renewable energy in EA Credit 2. Like EA Credit 1, these points are awarded on a sliding scale. If your project produces 2.5 percent of your total energy onsite, you get one point; if you produce 7.5 percent, you get two points; and if you produce 12.5 percent of the total energy used onsite, you get three points. LEED is not picky about *how* you generate this renewable energy, just that you *do* generate it. Your design can potentially use more popular tactics such as solar panels and wind, or branch out into less common strategies such as biomass, low-impact hydropower, or bio-gas. The obvious intent is to move as many buildings as possible off the traditional fossil fuel and power plant grid.

As mentioned before, the energy model that your team puts together for the design project will be measured against what is seen as "standard" for that building type in your climate and region—the baseline case or benchmark. The benchmarked energy level for your building can be found either through the modeling done in EA Credit 1 or from a document created by the U.S. Department of Energy (DOE)'s Energy Information Administration (EIA), called the 2003 Commercial Sector Average Energy Costs by State. This document is used in concert with the Commercial Buildings Energy Consumption Survey (CBECS), which addresses usage annually per square foot. (The LEED rating systems frequently make reference to such documents as a source of further information, so be ready to do your homework!) The numbers give you the total energy your building will use, to which the percentages listed above refer in order to determine the points you achieve for including onsite renewable energy generation in your design.

There are a few strategies that your design team may be tempted to include under these onsite energy credits; however, some of these strategies may be more beneficially applied to a different credit. The strategies referred to here are primarily passive, e.g., daylighting and thermal mass and architectural features such as exterior shading. While these strategies do ultimately affect the energy load of your design, they do it by lessening the energy needed as a whole and therefore are not applicable here and more properly incorporated into EA Credit 1.

Onsite Renewable Energy: LEED will not grant onsite renewable credits for some energy-producing systems such as ground source heat pumps or purchasing renewable power from offsite generation. The onsite renewable credit asks that each individual building help lighten its own footprint on the earth by providing for itself and embracing self-sufficiency. Options such as purchasing green energy from utilities still rely on others. And, while pulling renewable energy from the grid is definitely preferable to purchasing power from a coal-burning plant, the focus of this credit clearly advocates for onsite energy generated from renewable sources.

You can also receive one credit for purchasing renewable energy from other sources. EA Credit 6 rewards your project for specifying the use of grid-provided renewable energy for at least 35 percent of your building's necessary power needs. Again, you would establish this number either through the energy modeling completed in EA Credit 1 or by using the DOE's Commercial Buildings Energy Consumption Survey referenced earlier. The project must commit to the determined amount of renewable energy to be purchased through a two-year renewable energy contract that supplies at least 35 percent of the building's requirements.

If your project team is really dedicated to using renewable energy options, it is feasible that you could achieve the three points from producing 12.5 percent of your required energy onsite in EA Credit 2 (as previously discussed) and also receive the additional one point for entering into a two-year contract to purchase the 35 percent of grid-supplied renewable energy. This combination would net you a total of four points and give you the satisfaction of knowing your project has lightened its demand on the traditional coal-burning plant by nearly 50 percent.

2.9.5 Improving Refrigeration Management

Refrigeration management is a potentially scary-sounding topic of consideration under LEED. It need not be. Basically, refrigeration management means cutting down your building's contributions to global warming by eliminating chlorofluorocarbons (CFCs) and other harmful substances. If you have not heard of CFCs in reference to global warming or HVAC systems of the past, CFCs are chlorine-based compounds that have historically been used in aerosols, cleaning agents, blowing agents, and coolants such as those used in residential and commercial HVAC systems. CFCs were developed in the 1930s and later found to be detrimental to the ozone layer in the 1970s. The U.S. Food and Drug Administration and Environmental Protection Agency launched a phase-out of CFCs in 1976.

The Enhanced Refrigeration Management credit (EA 4) addresses a variety of possibilities you can use to reduce the impact of refrigeration on the atmosphere. With the help of your engineers, your building's refrigeration cycle can be engineered to minimize its impact on global warming through the selection of certain equipment and heating and cooling methods. If the designed building is cooled through passive strategies, this credit is just within your reach since your mechanical equipment, and therefore chemical coolants, are minimized. Note that HCFCs and halon (other refrigerants that helped to replace CFCs) can also be found hiding in your fire protection systems. These are not viewed as environmentally friendly either; don't let those systems steal the point out from under you!

2.10 Materials and Resources

The Materials and Resources category, affectionately known as MR, is exceptionally large in scope—much larger than you might think before you start digging into the particulars. In line with the interdisciplinary aspect of LEED and green building in general, MR ranges from the use of recycled content and regional materials, to managing waste on the construction site, to collecting recyclables in the finished, occupied building. The Materials and Resources credits are as follows:

- Prerequisite 1   Storage and Collection of Recyclables
- Credit 1   Building Reuse
- Credit 2   Construction Waste Management
- Credit 3   Materials Reuse
- Credit 4   Recycled Content

- Credit 5 Regional Materials
- Credit 6 Rapidly Renewable Materials
- Credit 7 Certified Wood

The Materials and Resources credits are the ones with which the architects and designers on your team are likely to be most comfortable. As it is typically their role to select the exterior and interior finishes, this category logically falls predominantly into their scope. However, as you are striving for a fully interdisciplinary team, you will immediately notice that there are credits within this category that will need the cooperation of others in the group. For example, construction waste management can be detailed in your specifications, but still needs to be executed onsite by the general contractors—who in turn need to educate all of their subcontractors. It can be a substantial chain to address if you are not looking for it. Similarly, engineers will need to be involved in some of the other credits, as they, too, specify materials that will be placed within the completed building. Fundamentally, though, these credits deal with how much material your team is using, where those materials come from, and what happens to the residual scraps as the construction takes place.

2.10.1 Recycling and Waste Management

As you might guess before you even look at anything remotely related to LEED guidelines, recycling is definitely a part of the package. If members of the general public know only one thing about doing their own part to save the environment, it is that they should be recycling! With this in mind, the only prerequisite in the Materials and Resources section is to enable and encourage the future users of the building to engage more easily in the recycling effort. To do this, the project must incorporate accessible and well-marked recycling collection locations throughout the facility for common recyclable materials, including cardboard, glass, paper, plastic, and metals. This covers most of the applicable materials in a typical office building, educational facility, hospitality venue, or retail location. Other programs, especially those including industrial facilities, need different arrangements for their recycling.

In addition to the nodes of collection stations throughout the design, there also must be a central storage space to gather these recyclables while they are waiting to be picked up. This is important and frequently overlooked. Make sure there is a specific space allocated for storage somewhere with easy access, such as in the basement or at the loading dock, in line with the LEED space requirements that allow the collected materials either to be taken on a daily basis or to await weekly removal.

You must also adhere to guidelines regarding daily waste removal on the construction site. Construction waste management is addressed in MR Credit 2 and can be good for up to two points (refer particularly to MR Credits 2.1 and 2.2). Similar to the energy performance and renewable energy credits in the Energy and Atmosphere section, these two possible credits are on a graduated scale. The goal of these two credits is to divert a good portion of construction waste from landing at the local landfill or being burned in incinerators. The first point can be achieved if 50 percent of construction waste is redirected to recycling or reuse, while two points can be achieved if 75 percent of the construction waste is redirected. The percentage of diversion is measured in weight, not cost, so keep that in mind as you ration out what goes where and to whom.

The construction materials identified by the LEED guidelines include the usual suspects—e.g., cardboard, glass, and plastic—but also extend to construction materials, including brick, metal, concrete, insulation, carpet, acoustical ceiling tile, gypsum wall board, and clean wood. Functionally speaking, there are a few different ways to encourage achieving this credit. One is to provide a number of different dumpsters on the construction site, each labeled for a different material, making it easier to sort onsite. Providing there is a decent amount of educating the subcontractors on the job about what they need to do and why, the different trades should certainly be able to find their way to dumping the correct material in the correct bin. Yet are many stories about how the architect, the head contractor, or the LEED point person visiting the construction site has had to physically lower themselves into dumpsters to "assist" in the separation of materials because those onsite are not complying without supervision. It is up to your team to encourage acceptance and adherence to this rule, or it simply will not work.

Another, simpler tactic for achieving these credits is to throw everything into one dumpster and have it sorted later offsite. That is easier and less time consuming for those onsite (and likely less expensive for you or your LEED AP than replacing pants and shoes ruined while sorting through a dumpster). In many locations there are actually companies that you can hire to come get your dumpsters, haul them away, and sort through the materials offsite. The cost for this is typically less than the dump fee at the landfill, which usually measures by weight, and the contractor may be refunded some of the cost depending on the material being recycled. While ultimately (although not necessarily) there may be more hauling involved, that is typically an acceptable trade-off for keeping the material out of the landfill. And who knows? Perhaps your trucks will be running on biofuel.

2.10.2 Reuse

Embodied energy is another concern for the green building movement, though it is more difficult to quantify and understand. A little background information: embodied energy is the amount of energy used to get a material to the point of being usable. This includes the energy used in:

- Extraction, such as the energy used for the chainsaw or bulldozer removing trees, or the mining machinery used to burrow down and extract precious metals;

- Transportation of the material to the mill for wood or the steel mill for metals;
- Manufacturing, which may include a kiln for certain bricks, or manufacturing plants for ducts, tubes, cables, and other equipment parts;
- Assembly of those parts (generally following a second round of transportation to the site), which include even small devices such as power screwdrivers to assemble HVAC units and resources used to pump water to mix the cement; and
- Installation, which may consist of concerns similar to those of assembly, and others including forklifts, table saws, and nail guns.

There is an enormous amount of energy—embodied energy—involved in the extraction, manipulation, delivery, and installation of every product involved in construction. Understanding that makes it clear that it is much more energy efficient for us to reuse materials that have already had embodied energy poured into them once than to send them to their eternal resting place in a landfill. That is the fundamental issue underlying the emphasis on reuse of materials.

A good way to harness already invested embodied energy is to look at the main structure of the design. MR Credit 1, Building Reuse, is broken into three possible parts: MR Credit 1.1, MR Credit 1.2, and MR Credit 1.3. These deal with using an existing structure rather than starting from scratch. Think of all the embodied energy that has been literally poured into the foundation, structure, and skin of existing buildings. Why not capitalize on those energy deposits? Should that indeed be your decision, and you encourage your client to renovate or inhabit an already existing structure, this credit will reward your project for that decision.

Just as construction waste materials use a graduated scale for achieving credits, so too does the reuse of embodied energy. Your project will get one credit if you maintain 75 percent of an existing structure's present walls, floors, and roof. Similarly, you will get an additional point (for a total of two) if you retain 95 percent of the existing floors, walls, and roof. If you really feel that you deserve a gold star, you can get one more point (three total) if you also retain 50 percent of the interior, nonstructural walls, doors, floors, floor coverings, etc. The more you keep, the more you gain. Not to mention, the more you keep, the less your client has to spend. We all know that clients who keep their money are happy clients. So, while this approach might result in a lower fee for you and your design team colleagues on the project at hand, a happy client could turn out to be your best source of referrals and repeat business.

More emphasis on reuse is encouraged by MR Credit 3, Materials Reuse, which is also split into two parts: MR Credit 3.1

and MR Credit 3.2. Here your team is encouraged to head out to the salvage yards or your local Habitat for Humanity Reuse Warehouse and find those gems that are still looking for a new home. Unlike the structural and other elements that were already within the building (just discussed), these reused elements come from elsewhere. The dual goal is still the same: to reduce the amount of product ultimately sent to the landfill, while also reducing the amount of embodied energy going into a project.

Products and materials that can be used for this credit are typically objects in and of themselves, like doors and windows, cabinets and millwork, stone slabs, paneling, brick, decorative elements, and beams or columns. Rescued from salvage yards and reuse warehouses, these items contribute to accruing points in this category. Mechanical, electrical, and plumbing pieces and parts need not apply. It is probable that the increase in efficiency seen between older models with the possibility of reuse and that of the newer models is not ultimately worth the reuse of such items.

Unlike the construction waste management credits that are based on weight, these credits are based on cost within the framework of the entire project. This can be documented by using a simple spreadsheet and keeping track of your receipts. Your project will get one credit for using salvaged materials totaling at least 5 percent of the total value of materials on the project, and a second point if your salvaged and reused materials constitute 10 percent of the total value of materials.

2.10.3 Product Origin

The third big concept found in the Materials and Resources section looks at the origin of the specified products for your project. The most obvious source in this category is local and regional materials. Remember the discussion of embodied energy? Product origin is a factor in that conversation because specifying materials of local origin cuts down on the travel necessary from product origin to end-use application.

MR Credit 5, Regional Materials, is another two-parter: MR Credit 5.1 and MR Credit 5.2. These credits ask you to favor building products that are extracted, processed, and manufactured regionally. Note that LEED currently defines "regionally" as within 500 miles, so mark your location on a map and get out that compass. Within that 500-mile radius is where you should be looking for your suppliers. If 10 percent of your materials (again based on cost) come from within that circle, you get one point. If 20 percent are extracted, processed, and manufactured within that circle, you will get two points. It's as simple as that. Again, this credit is based on total construction cost, not on weight. The lesson here: make sure you know where your materials are coming from.

2.10.4 Anatomy of the Material

Recycled content is another material concern that looks at where the products come from compositionally, in addition to the geographic consideration. What actually goes into your product? This relates to the concern about embodied energy by emphasizing and encouraging reduced environmental impacts by *not* extracting and processing more virgin materials. If your selected products can be based on previously used fibers or metals, then less needs to be pulled from dwindling resources. Not only would the resources stay intact longer, there would be less energy spent by eliminating the harvesting activity. Think of all the scarring of the earth and emissions that could be avoided if we did not have to go after additional resources. All this accomplished simply by finding materials containing recycled content.

Like the other split credits, the points are divided. One point can be achieved by ensuring that the post-consumer recycled content and one-half of pre-consumer recycled con-

---

Pre-consumer and Post-consumer: *These are two different types of recycled materials that LEED and other recycling programs specify. Post-consumer material is that which you recycle after you have purchased something—e.g., aluminum, cardboard, glass, etc. Pre-consumer material is usually a by-product of the industrial process. Such material is collected at the manufacturing or industrial site and sent back for integration into another product. Pre-consumer content is frequent in the carpet industry, for example.*

---

tent make up at least 10 percent of the total value of materials within the project (again based on cost, not weight). An additional point can be earned if the total achieves 20 percent of the total value of materials in the project.

When specifying products to gain recycled content credit, it is wise to be cautious about vendors' claims. Many vendors come in with samples and claim that their product can get you those recycled content points. Not so fast! It is very possible that that particular product might *contribute* to the total amount of recycled content you'll need to achieve the credit, but unless you plan on constructing your walls, floors, cabinetry, and ceilings out of carpet, for instance, it's unlikely to get you all the way there. Think closely about what you are told and how your selection of that material will actually translate into points. (Remember, no vendor or product is LEED certified, though they may be USGBC members and use the logo.) Each material will likely only contribute to your overall recycled content, not gain you the point all on its own. Remember to look at the complete picture.

2.10.5 Regeneration and Rotation
The last two credits in the Materials and Resources category, Rapidly Renewable Materials and Certified Wood, also address where the materials are coming from, but not geographically or compositionally. Instead, they look at the life cycle of the material itself and the crop management of wood.

While many natural resources are fundamentally renewable, it is the rate of their regeneration that is of concern here. For instance, the earth could create more coal—in millions and millions of years. This time frame, of course, essentially decrees coal a finite resource, as are many other resources used on a regular basis.

LEED, however, targets a much shorter time frame—not millions of years, but a single decade. LEED defines rapidly renewable resources as those that can be harvested in a ten-year cycle. Materials in this category include bamboo and cork, which can be harvested in three to five years and nine years, respectively. The flip side of these materials that have quick turnaround are old-growth forests and rainforests that take hundreds of years or more to replace. Other rapidly renewable resources are wool, linoleum, wheatboard, and cotton. The use of each of these in place of other materials lightens the burden on resources that have longer replenishment cycles, such as wood from old-growth forests and rainforests—resources that could easily be depleted. MR Credit 6, Rapidly Renewable Materials, allows for one point for the use of rapidly renewable materials for 2.5 percent of the total value (on a cost basis) of all materials and products used on the job.

Closely related to this is the basic notion of crop rotation in forests. As noted above, using old-growth wood resources is not the most environmentally friendly practice out there, and is definitely not advocated or suggested within the green building movement. Instead, the rating system is looking for environmentally responsible forest management—crop rotation and responsible land use—to ensure that the preferred types of wood are being harvested in an environmentally and socially responsible manner, respecting not only the history and integrity of the trees themselves but also the cultures and societies surrounding them, as well as the market relying on fair forest harvesting practices.

Targeted in MR Credit 7, Certified Wood, the whole process of wood certification, beginning to end, can be substantiated by a variety of different organizations. The most popular is the Forest Stewardship Council (FSC), which certifies forests, species, and management practices throughout the world. FSC is favored by LEED, and is referred to directly in the guidelines in MR Credit 7. To achieve this one point, 50 percent of all wood-based materials used in the project need to be FSC certified. This covers all wood elements including, but certainly not limited to, framing, subflooring, finished flooring, doors, and other architectural elements permanently installed in the project.

The Materials and Resources section is heavy with procurement and specification information, but none of it is insurmountable if you are armed with a little foresight and research. The design team should be closely integrated so that the contractor and subcontractors understand the importance of the specifications of a certain material—why that exact specification was selected and the importance of where (and who) it is coming from. The earlier everyone gets in the same room, the easier it will be to maneuver through these intricacies.

2.11 Indoor Environmental Quality

The last heavily weighted category is the Indoor Environmental Quality section (EQ), and it is substantial. This category offers the possibility of fifteen potential points in Version 2.2, some easier than others to earn. Unlike other more obvious categories, this one is not subject matter that is traditionally covered in design school—or anywhere else for that matter. In a way, it tries to address some of the concerns about Sick Building Syndrome (SBS). Though it's difficult, if not impossible, to nail down exactly what SBS is, the simplest definition is that people get sick when they are in certain buildings. This could occur for any number of reasons, from mold to bad air circulation to chemicals in the air. Often, indoor air is more polluted than outdoor air.

In line with this concern, what is the biggest expense for a company on a yearly basis? New carpet tiles? No. Copier maintenance? No. It is, in fact, the employees themselves. If the employees in a building are not feeling well or feel sluggish or take sick days, productivity goes down. The impact of poor environmental quality is most immediately human, of course, but it also takes what can amount to a huge toll on a company's bottom line. The Indoor Environmental Quality category in the rating system attempts to combat these concerns. The credits are as follows:

- Prerequisite 1   Minimum Indoor Air Quality Performance
- Prerequisite 2   Environmental Tobacco Smoke (ETS) Control
- Credit 1   Outdoor Air Delivery Monitoring
- Credit 2   Increased Ventilation
- Credit 3   Construction Indoor Air Quality Management Plan—During Construction; Before Occupancy
- Credit 4   Low-Emitting Materials—Adhesives and Sealants; Paints and Coatings; Carpet Systems; Composite Wood and Agrifiber Products
- Credit 5   Indoor Chemical and Pollutant Source Control
- Credit 6   Controllability of Systems—Lighting; Thermal Comfort
- Credit 7   Thermal Comfort—Design; Verification
- Credit 8   Daylighting and Views—Daylight 75% of Spaces; Views for 90% of Spaces

As you can see, many of these credits deal with fresh air, chemicals or off-gassing of materials, and the personal comfort and pleasure of individual occupants. While it is difficult to measure happiness of being in a space, there are plenty of studies indicating that natural daylight and views are preferred and beneficial. Occupant health and well-being is what this category is all about.

2.11.1 Ventilation

The first overarching issue addressed in the EQ section is ventilation and fresh air. The two prerequisites for the category and the first two credits deal primarily with getting fresh air to the occupants. While the first prerequisite asks that the HVAC system meet ASHRAE 62.1-2004 regarding overall ventilation rates, the second deals with possible infiltration of tobacco smoke into the otherwise fresh air of the building.

One of the options for the second prerequisite asks the design team to ensure that the building is smoke-free. The second part of this option asks the team to confirm that the outdoor smoking areas are minimum distances away from doors, operable windows, and outdoor air intakes. It would not do well to ask those who smoke to step outside, then locate their designated smoking area in front of an intake vent and proceed to pump the newly smoke-enhanced "fresh" air back into the building. Surprisingly, this has been done.

There are other options for the tobacco smoke prerequisite, including the creation within the building of designated smoking areas that are directly exhausted to the exterior. This eliminates the possibility of smoke mingling with the fresh air being delivered to the rest of the building. For residential buildings only, the credit requires prohibiting smoking in all common areas of the building, combined with a few other strategies regarding sealing the private units and possible air leakage.

While the second prerequisite aims to reduce the contamination of fresh air in the building by tobacco smoke, the first actual credit of the EQ section addresses the quality of air being delivered, probably from the outside, by advocating the use of carbon monoxide monitors and airflow rate monitors to keep tabs on the quality of the air and its velocity. This credit is also in the verification vein of LEED guidelines, making sure that equipment is doing what it is supposed to do. In this case, is the HVAC equipment delivering the required ventilation rates? An additional point can be earned in EQ Credit 2 by increasing the outdoor air ventilation rates by at least 30 percent. This added measure will enhance the indoor air quality for the occupants, ideally increasing productivity, well-being, and contentment.

2.11.2 Unhealthy Air

The second major theme of the EQ section is actual clean air. The goal is to get as many contaminants out of our indoor air as possible. Contaminants can come from a number of places, many that we have not traditionally considered. By understanding the masked carriers of air pollutants, design teams can greatly increase the health and happiness of building occupants.

Perhaps the most obvious contributor to airborne chemicals and particulates is the equipment housed in our offices. The common culprit is the copier machine, frequently multiple machines. Not only do they often emit a less-than-pleasant odor when they have been running, many also emit tiny particulates that can be inhaled and aggravate asthma and allergies. In EQ Credit 5, Outdoor Chemical and Pollutant Source Control, LEED suggests that the design team create separate, exhausted spaces for housing these machines where a negative pressure—essentially suction—can be created. That way, the chemicals are drawn up from the machines and into the exhaust system for the room rather than escaping into the rest of the work area.

Possibly the biggest and most under-recognized perpetrator of poor indoor air quality, however, are the materials the design team specifies to be brought into the building. We may not think about it much, but there are a number of materials which off-gas, and these can combine to raise the levels of contaminants throughout the space. Off-gassing is very similar to the new car smell that many people actually enjoy. But in actuality the smell comes from chemicals given off by the new materials in the car that have not had a chance to air out. The same goes for carpet, paints, and sealants that are specified in our buildings, to name just a few sources. The EQ Credits 4.1 through 4.4 look at these materials and what levels of volatile organic compounds (VOCs) they contain. Depending on the material, there is a list of VOC not-to-exceed levels intended to mitigate the offensive levels of chemicals brought into the building. The materials that LEED for New Construction identifies are:

- Adhesives: carpet glue, subfloor adhesives, cove base adhesives, structural wood member adhesives, etc.
- Sealants: architectural, roof membranes, etc.
- Paints: primers, paints, coatings, etc.
- Coatings: stains, sealers, varnishes, etc.
- Carpet Systems: padding, carpet, and adhesives
- Composite Wood and Agrifiber Products: MDF, particleboard, plywood, door cores, etc.

All of these materials can contaminate your project's indoor air quality if they are not appropriately monitored. Make sure that the design team has these substances in mind from the beginning and can incorporate the material requirements and levels that need to be met into the specifications book. It is a good idea to require submittals of these materials so the team can verify the VOC content of the various parts and pieces. During construction it is helpful to repeatedly mention the importance of ordering the right finishes, or even have someone come in and do a training session for your contractors if they have not been through the LEED process before. It is best to make sure all your bases are covered so that nothing seemingly routine—such as sealants, paints, or carpet—slips through the cracks on your project.

> **Volatile Organic Compounds (VOCs):** *According to the U.S. Environmental Protection Agency (www.epa.gov/iaq/voc.html), VOCs are harmful gasses secreted by different solid or liquid materials. Common materials such as paints, paint thinners, cleaning supplies, pesticides, fabricated furnishings, copiers and printers, glues and adhesives, markers, carpeting, varnish, formaldehyde in wood, and pre-finished doors are common culprits. The fumes can cause eye, nose, and throat irritation; headaches; nausea; damage to the liver, kidney, and central nervous system; and, potentially cancer.*

2.11.3 Occupant Comfort

The last major part in the EQ section is occupant comfort, plain and simple. How many times have you been stuck in a room that is either sweltering or frigid, with no idea how to adjust it to a comfortable temperature? Or a room where the windows do not latch and just blow and flap, regardless of the weather outside? Or have no windows at all, so you had no idea what time of day it was? Have you had glare from an overhead light shining on your screen when there was plenty of natural light so that electric lights didn't even need to be on? If these are familiar situations, Occupant Comfort will be a category near and dear to your heart.

Indoor Environmental Quality tries its best to ensure that occupants are comfortable and able to manage their environment to enhance the level of comfort. EQ Credits 6.1 and 6.2, Controllability of Systems, deal with the ability to personally control both the lighting and the thermal systems of spaces. The lighting credit advocates for decent levels of ambient light, while emphasizing the importance of individually controlled light sources such as personal task lighting and desk lamps. It is essential to understand the actual lighting needs of the client and work with those requirements to determine appropriate lighting strategies.

The second part of the controllability of systems is the credit relating to thermal comfort. This one is a little trickier, but still manageable. For mechanical systems, there may be the option to combine the traditional mechanical system with the use of operable windows (which may help the design team with some ventilation credits as well). Appropriate zoning of different spaces for the mechanical system is also a valid approach. Beyond that, there are the options of individual room thermostat controls, local and operable vents at the floor of systems furniture, or other thermal comfort systems. All of these strategies can help achieve an acceptable level of occupant-specific comfort.

The actual design (as opposed to control) of the thermal comfort systems is not left behind in the LEED checklist; two possible points are associated with them. EQ Credits 7.1 and 7.2, Thermal Comfort, are based on ASHRAE codes intent on achieving thermal comfort and quality for the occupants. The first credit looks at the design of the HVAC systems, emphasizing the ASHRAE Standard 55-2004, Thermal Comfort Conditions for Human Occupancy. Essentially, LEED is looking for a well-designed envelope and systems that can deliver a space of quality and standardized range of comfort. These include measurements of air velocity, radiant temperature, air temperature, and relative humidity. This is not to be confused with the controllability credit discussed for EQ 6.1 and 6.2; EQ 7.1 and 7.2 provide for a standardized comfort range, while the previous credits pertain to the modification and fine-tuning of the comfort strategies.

The second credit surrounding thermal comfort looks for proof that the designed system is performing as intended. It is the ever-present verification credit. This credit requests an occupant survey between six and eighteen months after the building is occupied to ensure that the occupants are indeed comfortable. If the results show that more than 20 percent of occupants are dissatisfied, a plan must be developed to fix whatever they have determined is not working correctly.

Daylight and views are important not only because they create a pleasurable space but also because they contribute to the control function. EQ Credits 8.1 and 8.2, Daylight and Views, deal with this visual access to the natural environment. The first credit considers how many spaces have natural daylighting and sets 75 percent of the spaces as the threshold for receiving credit for this feature. There are a number of ways to validate that this level has been met. The verification options include calculations (a minimum glazing/glass factor of 2 percent in at least 75 percent of all regularly occupied spaces), computer simulations, and daylight measurements. Specifications and additional requirements are outlined in the Reference Guide, but this gives you an understanding of the intent. Not only do naturally lit spaces improve morale, they have also been crediting for improving productivity.

Views are also typically seen as a favorable element in designs. Not many people want to spend their days feeling as if they were holed up in a bunker. LEED looks for 90 percent of regularly occupied spaces to have views. Clerestory glass and skylights may be able to help you in the daylighting credit, but for the view portion of this credit, LEED is looking for vision glazing (windows you can see out of) located between 2'6" and 7'6" above the finished floor. Again, there are calculations needed to actually achieve this credit, but the intent is obvious. It campaigns for lower partitions, fewer private offices, and interior glazing to allow views from interior spaces. It can be problematic if the client is set on rows of private offices along the exterior of the building, but the interior and exterior wall material might be manipulated enough to still allow views. While we all know the torture of being inside on a beautiful day and not being able to go out and enjoy it, wouldn't anyone still rather see that it is there than be holed up?

2.11.4 Construction Management

The last issue addressed in the EQ section is the notion of construction indoor air quality management, Credits 3.1 and 3.2. This is going to be predominantly in the hands of the contractor on your team, but it is always a good thing to address up front with everything else. The idea here is that the contractor manages the site to help minimize any situations that could contribute to bad indoor air quality later on. There are two phases to this: during construction and before occupancy.

LEED asks that the contractor formulate a process plan during construction to address any standard procedures or approaches that could lead to bad air quality down the road. For example, if the drywall subcontractor brings in stacks of drywall that are stored under a tarp outside or near an open exterior façade, there is a good chance that these stacks of drywall would get wet at some point. If they get wet, they may dry. But what if they start to grow little bits of mold instead? Then they are installed and painted over, mold and all. That mold will not help the indoor air quality. Other absorptive materials that could cause the same problem include insulation, ceiling tile, and carpeting.

Another potential problem area is the installation of ductwork. As the process traditionally goes, the structure is put up and ductwork is installed, followed closely by the construction of the interior walls. That means the ducts are installed and sitting there while the drywall is being cut and drywall dust is floating here and there. Among the places it will likely settle is inside those ducts. When they get turned on after the client moves in, all that drywall dust will be raining down on the newly situated employees. Mess aside, this is definitely not good for lungs! A way to guard against this unfortunate event is to seal the ducts after they are in place, while the rest of the construction is charging forward. Limiting the dirt and dust that gets into the air passage leaves the final building cleaner and healthier.

The second phase of the construction indoor air quality management deals with a cleansing of sorts before occupancy. This helps deal with any dust that has gathered or off-gassing that has occurred during the construction process and tries to get it cleared out before people actually move into their space. One option is to flush out the building. This essentially runs increased ventilation through the spaces to try to rid them of any leftover smells, particles, or gasses that may linger. Think about driving with your windows down to get rid of the new car smell. Flushing is similar to that, on a much bigger scale. Another option is to do air quality testing. It may be that a flush-out is not needed if the contaminant and chemical levels are low enough to meet the guidelines. Which option to choose for achieving this credit depends on how well the issue has been managed during construction, as well as the materials used in the design.

As we have seen, the Indoor Environmental Quality section

of LEED for New Construction is all about the health and well-being of the occupants. This encompasses both the physical aspects (such as allergies and asthma, as addressed by the construction management and VOC credits) and the mental well-being of occupants (addressed by the controllability of systems and exposure to daylight and views). In this way, LEED tries to address the impact of the construction industry not only on the environment itself but also on the occupants who inhabit those buildings—you and me!

2.12 Innovation in Design

Technically, the last credit category is the Innovation in Design (ID) category. None of these credits are required, and historically there has been only the possibility of achieving five points—although in LEED 2009 that goes up to six possible points. One of the points is available for having a LEED Accredited Professional on the design team, integral to the process and project. That credit is so simple that it's a no-brainer. For the remaining four points under Version 2.2 (five under LEED 2009), the idea of the ID category is to allow design teams to be creative with sustainability and green building by looking for alternatives that (1) go beyond the targets of some of the credits by illustrating *exceptional* performance and/or (2) are not covered in the LEED rating system as it currently stands.

For example, an innovation point could be received by achieving a 40 percent water savings, as opposed to simply the 20 or 30 percent stipulated in the credits. The LEED rating system rewards your team for going above and beyond the objective. The other popular option for innovation credits is including items not covered in the rating system. Examples of this would be educational signage pointing out green strategies used in the building; green cleaning initiatives for housekeeping that standardize maximum allowable uses of VOCs and chemicals; educational tours of the building open to the public; or low-emitting furniture within the space, contributing to better air quality. While none of these is specifically enumerated or addressed in the rating system or reference guide, they are obviously steps toward better environments for users.

Because a number of these credits, like those listed above, were being submitted over and over again for different projects, USGBC released a document in early 2008 that listed established and generally approved initiatives and strategies that would likely count for ID credits. By doing this, they were able not only to encourage some of these practices as established but also to standardize the criteria that would need to be met if a certain point was desired.

To see how this works, let's look at the Green Cleaning credit. While there is not currently a credit in the standard LEED Rating System for this process requests for using this procedure for Innovation credits have been so frequent that USGBC has created criteria and identified required submittals. Green Cleaning is now outlined with requirements such as including a "final clean-up by an independent green cleaning service using cleaning products that meet the Green Seal GS-37 standard, floor cleaners complying with CA Code of Regulations maximum VOC content, and disposable paper products, supplies, and trash bags meeting the minimum requirements of the U.S. EPA's Comprehensive Procurement Guidelines." One of the submittal requirements is a "Description of contractual and procedural requirements for operations staff including training and implementation." This shows how a previously vague issue has been herded into a viable and verifiable strategy.

2.13 Discussions About USGBC and LEED

While LEED is clearly the most well-known and widely used green building rating system across the United States and almost certainly the world, there are concerns with and arguments against both the organization and its products. These range from issues with point allocation to issues with the organization itself. Below you'll find a brief discussion of a few issues that seem to come up most frequently.

2.13.1 Frequently Voiced Concerns

One of the most commonly heard concerns about the organization and its rating systems is the idea that LEED certification is seen as the primary goal. A number of academics and practitioners vehemently argue that to design really sustainable buildings we must go beyond LEED to another level. They claim that LEED allows practitioners to stop short of pushing the boundaries, where they feel green building really must go to achieve a healthy relationship between construction and the environment.

The Energy and Atmosphere category may be the most widely contested group of credits within the rating systems; many critics view LEED's stance on energy reduction and energy efficiency marginal at best. In a world where energy debates are at the forefront of everyone's minds, requiring only a 14 percent efficiency increase (and that only recently) is viewed as an insufficient contribution to energy reduction. Some academics and practitioners are uneasy about the minimum energy credits needed to achieve a certified building, at times barely meeting the local energy code.

A common feeling among green architects and builders who have been doing this type of design for decades is that USGBC has set the bar too low in an effort to capture more of the market.

2.13.2 Response

In responding specifically to this technical issue, USGBC recently approved mandating a minimum of two Energy Optimization points in addition to the Minimum Energy Performance prerequisite. Projects registered after the date of this decision must achieve a minimum of two points to become certified.

As a general response to the above issue, USGBC feels that the LEED Green Building Rating System was developed to drive market transformation in the building industry by defining a consensus metric for leadership in green building that forms a basis for continuous improvement. LEED continues to evolve over the years based on technical, scientific, and market-based advancements. When LEED was introduced in 2000, it helped to spark a revolution that is changing the way we build and operate our offices, schools, hospitals, and homes. With its vision of a sustainable built environment for everyone within a generation, the USGBC is focused on mission-critical activities such as the development of LEED, educational programs, and the development and dissemination of tools that the construction and related industries need in order to address the most pressing issues of our time: global climate change, energy dependence, water issues, and human health. Without the LEED rating system there would not be nearly as much discussion surrounding the green building movement, discussion that is making it really a movement. The market transformation urged on by green builders and LEED has brought green building to the forefront. LEED will continue to reset the bar for green building leadership because the urgency of USGBC's mission has challenged the industry to move faster and reach further.

In closing this discussion of LEED, I would like to acknowledge that it simply is not possible to create a document so thorough that it addresses *all* issues that could possibly arise in every aspect of design and *all* varieties of construction. Many LEED advocates rightly see the rating systems as a vehicle to keep the topic of green building construction at the forefront of our concerns, and not as the be-all and end-all in rules. The LEED rating system has kept and continues to keep the discussion of green building lively and the market transformation urged on by green builders vibrant.

3: The Natural Step

the NATURAL STEP

Unlike other guideline and rating systems covered in this book, The Natural Step is a framework based on natural and social systems rather than on specific principles and concerns found in the construction industry. Although used most frequently by organizations in the manufacturing and service industries, The Natural Step is now being used successfully in the construction field in both Europe and the United States. Developed through a consensus process (which will be described below), The Natural Step establishes a framework for sustainability, the key feature of which is its science-based definition of a sustainable society articulated as four system principles or conditions. Organizations can use The Natural Step to understand how what they do fits within the larger environment, encouraging them to revisit their standard practices and to become more innovative and efficient.

3.1 Organization Overview

Frustrated by what he viewed as a disjointed approach to a growing and undeniable environmental crisis, the Swedish oncologist Dr. Karl-Henrik Robèrt engaged his medical and scientific networks in a process to establish a consensus view of the requirements for achieving a sustainable society. These efforts, begun in 1989 and facilitated by Dr. Robèrt, resulted in the creation of the framework named The Natural Step. Many of Sweden's leading scientists were involved in this process, which entailed an extensive operational review of Dr. Robèrt's first framework proposal for a sustainable society. All of the individuals involved in refining this vision worked toward consensus as they reviewed a series of drafts. The goal of this circular process was to ensure that all primary concerns were addressed and taken into consideration before the framework was adopted.

    Dr. Robèrt began by writing a scientific paper that outlined his ideas for a framework for sustainable society. He circulated the paper among more than thirty colleagues. As comments came back from these reviewers, Dr. Robèrt made refinements based on their comments and concerns. Some twenty-two drafts later, consensus was reached on some fundamental principles that make the earth's ecosystem function successfully—the guidelines now known as The Natural Step Framework. As

Systematic Thinking versus Systems Thinking: *Systematic thinking focuses on problem-solving through an organized, disciplined, practical, and analytical process. The term is often used to describe people who are logical and orderly in their thinking and problem-solving.* Systems thinking, *on the other hand, looks at problems in a part-to-whole relationship that is, essentially, more global in scope. By understanding the entire system, one gets a better and more useful perspective on the specific problem at hand. In the context of this book, the system in question, of course, is the environment. For more information on systems thinking, read Joseph O'Connor and Ian McDermott's* The Art of Systems Thinking: Essential Skills for Creativity and Problem-Solving *(for a general discussion) and Fritjof Capra's* The Web of Life: A New Scientific Understanding of Living Systems *(for systems thinking as applied to living systems).*

mentioned previously, the guidelines are based on scientific principles and systems thinking as they are illustrated in nature, then generalized into organizational principles designed to encourage the development of a sustainable society.

3.2 The Four System Conditions

While LEED and Green Globes (described in Chapter 4) have different categories of credits and processes, The Natural Step takes a different approach—one based on the four system conditions that form its framework. These four conditions are much broader in scope than those of other frameworks and rating systems. The basis of each condition is explained below, including its applicability to the building industry.

3.2.1 Condition 1

In order for a society to be sustainable, nature's functions and diversity are not systematically subject to increasing concentrations of substances extracted from the earth's crust.

Earth's ecosystem is being negatively affected by the amounts of certain metals and minerals being extracted from the earth's crust and deposited in the biosphere. Take fossil fuels as an example. Carbon-based fuels are extracted and burned today at a rate that elevates the concentration of carbon dioxide (CO_2) in the atmosphere without any time for self-correction. Mined materials—such as lead, cadmium, and copper—are another example. Even small spills or trace amounts of such elements left uncontained in the environment can do considerable damage as rain washes them into sewers and streams, contaminating the ecosystems and harming the organisms they touch along the way. Once the levels of these and other harmful extracted substances are elevated in the biosphere, they can take centuries or more to work their way down to what we think of as "normal" levels. We could certainly debate what is "normal" and what is "acceptable" regarding these levels, but rather than that, let's simply agree that "less is more."

As levels of these elements increase in the biosphere rapidly and continuously as a result of human extraction, the environment as a whole and individual ecosystems are unable to heal themselves adequately. Natural processes operate on geological time scales, not human ones, and thus cannot remove these substances as quickly as they accumulate. The levels of extraction and rapid use of these materials is undoubtedly on the rise. When the increases are combined with no time allowance for systems to heal themselves, the result includes such problems as groundwater contamination and climate change. In addition, the levels of heavy metals in our daily lives—including but not limited to copper, mercury, and cadmium—have increased. These metals can be found in any number of places—ocean water and aquifers, air, food, dust, waste sites, and even our daily workplaces. Although The Natural Step Framework has not drawn the following correlation, other organizations have produced scientific studies regarding how some of these trace substances may affect human life and well-being: symptoms of these substances in high concentrations can include DNA mutation, cancer, joint pain, drowsiness, Parkinson's disease, depression, and hypoglycemia. Per The Natural Step's Condition 1, sustainability requires that nature's systems not be disrupted by such unhealthy imbalances.

Implication for the Building Industry

How does Condition 1 affect the design and construction industries from a practical, applied standpoint? The goal of Condition 1 is to moderate harmful waste. Some elements are common and acceptable; others are more problematic. Condition 1 asks that those extracted materials that are problematic and are being used in construction be both accounted for and, preferably, contained in some way. In addition, The Natural Step recommends that materials of concern be used wisely and that, wherever possible, we search for suitable substitutes. What happens to fossil fuels "required" for construction equipment? What about the cadmium used in batteries, colored plastics, and specialty paints, or as stabilizers in PVC? Copper is used by electricians because of its high thermal and electrical conductivity and because it is much more affordable than silver. What happens to scraps or residuals used in creating these construction necessities? Do they end up in a landfill, permeating the ground and our lives?

Similarly, if containing carbon emissions, such as those created when burning fossil fuels, is unlikely based on our current standard practices, then the only possible choice is to stop using fossil fuels as the primary fuel source. Alternatives do exist and, as creative as the construction fields are, we ought to be able to find them. Though these issues may seem distant from the daily concerns of practitioners in the design and construction industries, they are issues that most definitely belong within our scope of consideration.

3.2.2 Condition 2
In order for a society to be sustainable, nature's functions and diversity are not systematically subject to increasing concentrations of substances produced by society.

In principle, this is very similar to the first condition. Both concern what types of additions the natural environment can and cannot handle. The emphasis of Condition 2, however, is on man-made substances that are created and then remain in the environment, such as DDT, CFC and HCFC refrigerants,

> **DDT:** *The scientific name for DDT is* dichlorodiphenyltrichloroethane, *once a popular pesticide for agriculture and disease-carrying insects. Although DDT was banned in 1972 because of its detrimental effects on wildlife (as emphasized in Rachel Carson's seminal book,* Silent Spring), *the chemical is still used in some countries today.*

DDT truck spraying beaches on Long Island in the 1940s to rid the area of mosquitos. © Bettmann/CORBIS

and PCBs. All are man-made and all are viewed as less than desirable.

PCBs, for example, are very persistent substances that hang on stubbornly in the environment, taking years to break down or dissipate. Not a product of any natural sources, PCBs are man-made combinations of up to hundreds of individual chlorinated compounds. The myriad forms they can take make them particularly difficult to control. Previous uses of PCBs have included heat transfer fluid, hydraulic fluid, dye car-

PCBs: *As noted on the Center for Disease Control's Agency for Toxic Substance and Disease Registry Web site (www. atsdr.cdc.gov), the official name for PCBs is actually poly-chlorinated biphenyls. PCBs are resistant, man-made, chlorinated compounds that can take many forms, including liquid, solid, or vapor. They permeate the environment, which makes them difficult to corral and eliminate.*

riers, and copy paper; PCBs are components in paints, adhesives, and caulking compounds. PCBs can enter the air, soil, and water during just about any phase of their manufacture, use, or disposal. They accumulate in bodies of water, plants, and animals, navigating up the food chain as smaller plants and animals become food for larger ones. The chemical arrives in our human bodies by way of the fish, dairy products, and meat we eat. PCBs are so pervasive that they have been found in breast milk and thus passed from mother to child. The most common effects of PCBs on humans are skin rashes, acne, and liver and kidney problems.

While manufacturing PCBs was banned in 1997 in the United States, these compounds are still embedded in many forms within our environment. For example, numerous electric transformers and capacitors created with PCBs are still used in the U.S. Similarly, PCBs are, even now, inadvertently produced as by-products in the manufacture of certain organic chemicals.

While PCBs are no longer a primary product, they still enter the environment in this way, as well as by means of foreign products imported for use in local processes and manufacturing.

We need not avoid all synthetic materials. Rather, materials that accumulate and linger in nature should be used sparingly and kept in closed-loop cycles.

Implication for the Building Industry

Much like Condition 1, Condition 2's scope seems a bit distant from daily concerns in the design and construction fields. Has anyone ever asked you about DDT in connection with your work? Probably not. But in the design and construction fields, synthetic materials are everywhere. Flame retardants, PVCs, paints and finishes, fabric content—all fall within this area.

As with the practical applications of Condition 1, the simplest lesson with respect to Condition 2 is to avoid certain types of synthetic substances in design specifications and the construction process. The question to ask is what need do such materials fulfill or what problem do they solve? There are a number of unnatural creations within the environment that only exist because humankind has created them to fill a need that we have also created. Are there other methods or products that can fill the need or solve the problem? That is what we should be seeking.

Condition 2 introduces the concept of life cycle analysis into The Natural Step Framework. How many different types of products are needed to make the conduit, the plastic laminate, or the stain-resistant carpet and backing under consideration for a project? This is the type of question to ask. We need to understand where our products are coming from and what gives them their qualities. As we specify materials and composite products, we need to think about everything that might go into the creation of the product, about the life of the product, and about the chemicals to which building occupants will be exposed. Finally, we must consider the product's end of life. What will happen to the carpet, the fabrics, the materials used when new tenant improvements are made? Some products can actually be "leased" these days. For example, some carpet manufacturers will pick up the used carpet, take it to be recycled, and replace the floor with new material—and continue to repeat the process when the time comes again.

3.2.3 Condition 3

In order for a society to be sustainable, nature's functions and diversity are not systematically impoverished by physical displacement, over-harvesting, or other forms of ecosystem manipulation.

While Condition 3, like Conditions 1 and 2, speaks to the tolerance levels of the natural environment, here The Natural Step starts to look at overuse and destruction of natural systems. It does not consider what is being added to the environment but rather what is being taken away. Its concern is the issues of over-harvesting and depletion of resources, for instance, in lumber acquisition and water use. Because finite resources are available on the planet, the design and construction industries must look carefully at the renewal process for each of these resources and focus considerable effort on not exhausting them. This will allow both present and future generations to continue enjoying them, either for true needs or simply for recreation. Condition 3 is also intended to foster understanding and support of acceptable resource harvest rates so that we extract and use resources at a sustainable rate—one that is appropriate for the species being used as well as for the ecosystem to which it belongs.

By extension, Condition 3 speaks to the larger ecosystems existing in nature. A major debate exists within the environmental ethics field regarding the rights of non-humans to their version of life.* The Natural Step Framework does not enter the debate regarding animal and species rights; instead, it assumes that we cannot interfere with natural systems in ways that would render them unable to replenish themselves. It may be that different fauna and flora are needed in each system, but The Natural Step Framework does not expressly address non-human rights, even though that argument could be made

---

*See Tom Regan's *The Case for Animal Rights* (University of California Press, 2004) and Tom Regan and Peter Singer's *Animal Rights and Human Obligations* (Prentice Hall, 1989).

through the application of Condition 3. Similar to this concern, but not directly related to The Natural Step, is the idea of "natural capitalism" as explained by Paul Hawken in his 1994 book *The Ecology of Commerce*. In a nutshell, the idea is that while anyone can go out into a forest and cut down a tree, there is a true value of that tree that is not being recognized. Not only is there a price of lumber that we may want to consider if it was taken from a lumber supplier, there are also a number of necessary services that the tree provides that are not taken into consideration in the cost of the tree. For example, the tree produces oxygen. How much would that service alone cost? It also provides shelter, filters water, creates habitat for other living things, produces food, and stabilizes the earth and soil. Where do these services get accounted for? Is this incorporated into the $3.46 cost for a 2" × 4" piece of Douglas fir? Similarly, marshlands contain, filter, and purify water before allowing it to percolate into the ground, replenishing groundwater. Plants purify and detoxify air through their natural systems, ridding the air of harmful substances embedded within it. None of these system costs are taken into account in the design and construction industries because we take these processes for granted.

Implication for the Building Industry

There are two primary practical suggestions for Condition 3 within the building industry. The first pertains to the informed uses of resources; the second concerns the impact that structures and development have on the land. Organizations that embrace The Natural Step as a foundation for encouraging better resource management—Interface Carpet, for example—are educating people about how their products embrace holistic sustainability to create socially beneficial and economically viable products.* By rolling its sustainably manufactured product out into commercial and residential venues, Interface Carpet helps to raise awareness about larger environmental issues within the marketplace. By recycling fibers, using low-VOC materials and dyes, and creating products and processes that generate no waste, this carpet company has shifted the expectations for the entire flooring industry. The company actually goes several steps further toward sustainability by agreeing to take back used carpet after its useful installed life and recycling it into the manufacturing process.

The popularity of recycled alternatives in materials such as glass and metals also speaks to resource management, both in industry and for the public in general. Understanding where the materials specified in the design process are harvested and manufactured is becoming increasingly important to members of the building industry. Even better is when we can use reclaimed or found materials rather than new ones, particularly in preference over traditionally "harvested" materials and

*See more at www.interfaceglobal.com

even in lieu of sustainably produced materials. This approach is a common theme in other standard green building guidelines, but within The Natural Step Framework it takes on a broader scope.

The second practical implication of Condition 3 within the building industry is how natural ecosystems are altered during the process of construction as well as throughout the life of the building. There is the obvious impact of clearing land and manipulating landforms and ecosystems so that the original landscape is unrecognizable. One alternative to this practice, of course, is to use a previously developed site or brownfield, minimizing the impact of further development on natural resources. Just as The Natural Step emphasizes the informed use of resources like green building guidelines, so too its strategy focuses on redevelopment and brownfield (as can be seen in the discussions of both LEED and Green Globes in this book).

Another example of altering the existing ecosystem during construction is the practice of covering a site with impervious surfaces such as roads, parking lots, and roofs that do not allow water to readily return to the ground. With enough impervious surfaces, the potential for flooding during heavy rains increases significantly. Flooding aside, the covered ground further alters not only the immediate construction site itself but also the landscape around it through the "butterfly effect." The idea of the "butterfly effect" is that even the smallest action in the atmosphere—such as a butterfly beating its wings—can activate a cause and effect chain of events that could potentially alter other happenings such as a tornado in a certain location. In addition, whatever problems the established construction site either has inherently or creates are literally sent downstream as rainwater flows to another site that may have been unaffected previously. Downstream ecosystems are disrupted; flora and fauna, having lost their homes, are displaced and sent to live somewhere else. It's much like how our trash goes away. It is not really our problem if it is out of sight and out of mind. Or is it?

Each of the two implications addressed in Condition 3 is detrimental on its own to the systems within the natural order, but together they have an exceptional impact. For example, rainwater gathers toxins from building materials as it hits their surfaces and is then routed directly to the watershed by way of the sewer without being given a chance (as would happen within the natural system) to be cleaned and detoxified in the ground. Similarly, the temperature of the air in the immediate vicinity increases through the heat island effect, but just a fraction of the plant life remains intact onsite to help mediate the effects. The result is not only the potentially severe loss in the overall quantity of plant life per se but also the mediation that these plants provide with respect to CO_2 levels and global warming. Combined, these issues make for one big environmental mess revolving around the established construction process.

3.2.4 Condition 4
In a sustainable society, people are not subject to conditions that systematically undermine their capacity to meet their needs.

Unlike the previous three conditions, which are related to natural systems' tolerances and their capacity to deal with alterations, Condition 4 speaks to the quality of human life. This condition recognizes that humans are an integral part of natural systems and that the way in which humans interact with one another impacts both human and natural systems.* The condition recognizes that society and business exist to meet human needs; how these needs are met is critical to social and environmental sustainability. It is important to note that there are a number of human needs, including subsistence, affection, protection, and participation with other people, which are met through interdependence, diversity (each person is unique), and self-organization.

Sustainable human systems require transparency, accountability, participation, and honesty. For example, as societies continue to pollute and contaminate, they may be, as stated by Condition 4, undermining their capacity to meet their own needs in the future. The implications of primarily business decisions (such as how a product is manufactured, what type of waste is created and dealt with, and what types of emissions are expelled into the local water and air) affect numerous populations, both adjacent to manufacturing sites and in other locales. It is the understanding and owning of this responsibility through the practices of transparency, accountability, participation, and honesty that Condition 4 sees as imperative.

Implication for the Building Industry
Condition 4 addresses a number of procedures in the building industry. First is the standardized process we use to design. Are designers talking with the local community to understand its wants and needs? In their formal education architects are given the foundation to understand and incorporate many of the human needs outlined in Condition 4, but how much are these needs really considered when pen is put to paper? What criteria are being used to select materials? Do the materials specified really take human needs into consideration? Are emissions and energy consumption being modeled and incorporated into these decisions?

Second, the policies underlying design decisions need to be thoroughly understood (and perhaps altered to better support sustainability). What type of parking is required by code? Does the jurisdiction in which the project is located allow greywater systems? Are there energy tax credits or other benefits

---

*For more on the debate surrounding if humans and our actions, surroundings and accessories are "natural," see the vast literature on the topic in the field of Environmental Ethics.

available for low-energy buildings, reducing the need for fossil fuels? Perhaps foremost should be discussions held by the client and design team regarding the priorities that sustainable practices will have within the project parameters. For example, will formaldehyde-filled products be selected over formaldehyde-free products because of the price point? Will ceiling fans be included to enhance passive ventilation even though they may compromise some forms of aesthetics? Every decision made in the design and construction process has implications and trade-offs. Condition 4 asks that we be aware of the circumstances created by our decisions throughout the entire process.

3.3 Translation into the Building Industry

In 1999, a construction industry task force was formed through the Oregon Natural Step Network (now simply the Natural Step Network) to look specifically at how Natural Step principles could be applied systematically to the construction of commercial buildings. Because the conditions of The Natural Step are so large and all-encompassing, it would be virtually impossible to translate them into prescriptive guidelines like LEED or Green Globes. Instead of focusing on steps or processes to get to a greener building, The Natural Step task force focused on really understanding the end goal of a thoroughly sustainable building. The team used a "backcasting" approach, first envisioning the end goal, then moving backward to understand how to get

there through the typical construction process.* The task force succeeded in coming up with requirements—called a "Full Alignment State"—for a building that would be in complete compliance with The Natural Step conditions, meaning that none of the four system conditions is violated. The example in the sidebar illustrates how this approach addresses the issues pertaining to materials selection, use, and disposal. As this breakdown shows, quantifiable strategies certainly exist that can be incorporated into construction practices to enable buildings and developments to adhere to the principles of The Natural Step. The task force also created a methodology for using The Natural Step's principles together with LEED. Architecture firms, green building consultants, engineering firms, construction firms, and developers are using this integrated design approach successfully.

3.4 Discussions About The Natural Step

To date, some notable organizations have used The Natural Step—among them IKEA, Interface, and Nike. Companies use this framework for a number of reasons, including to help them move beyond in-place regulations, improve stakeholder

---

*For the complete report of the Construction Industry Task Force, see the publication (Version 10, published October 2004) on the Natural Step Network Web site: www.thenaturalstep.org/en/using-natural-step-a-framework-toward-construction-and-operation-fully-sustainable-buildings

Construction Industry Task Force: Full Alignment State Guiding Principles for Material Selection, Use, and Disposal

1. *All materials are non-persistent, non-toxic, and procured either from reused, recycled, renewable, or abundant (in nature) sources.*

    a) *Reused means reused or remanufactured in the same form, such as remilled lumber, in a sustainable way.*

    b) *Recycled means the product is 100% recycled and can be recycled again in a closed loop in a sustainable way.*

    c) *Renewable means able to regenerate in the same form at a rate greater than the rate of consumption.*

    d) *Abundant means human flows are small compared to natural flows, i.e., aluminum, silica, iron, etc.*

    e) *In addition, the extraction of renewable or abundant materials has been accomplished in a sustainable way, efficiently using renewable energy and protecting the productivity of nature and the diversity of species.*

2. *Design and use of materials in the building will meet the following in order of priority:*

    a) *Material selection and design favor deconstruction, reuse, and durability appropriate to the service life of the structure.*

    b) *Solid waste is eliminated by being as efficient as possible, or*

    c) *Where waste does occur, reuses are found for it onsite, or*

    d) *For what is left, reuses are found offsite.*

    e) *Any solid waste that cannot be reused is recycled or composted.*

Source: "Using The Natural Step as a Framework Toward the Construction and Operation of Fully Sustainable Buildings," by the Oregon Natural Step Construction Industry Group. Retrieved from www.naturalstep.ca.

perceptions, integrate sustainable policies into the workplace, and reduce environmental risk and operating costs. In the green building arena, companies have used The Natural Step to design and build buildings that have achieved LEED Gold and Platinum ratings, such as the Oregon Health and Science University Center for Health and Healing.

While many other green building guidelines and frameworks concentrate on prescriptive strategies, specific approaches, and technologies applicable to the building design and construction process, The Natural Step, as previously noted, casts a wider net while still focusing on and marking the end goal. Suppose, for example, we are at point A (our current society) and want to get to point G (a sustainable society) by way of the building industry. Other guidelines address a particular process or specific applications and strategies. The guidelines may prescribe going through point B (regional materials) and possibly through point D (cross ventilation) and point E (a greywater system). In contrast, The Natural Step process allows you to envision your end point G via its four system conditions and leaves it up to you to decide how to get there. This perspective recognizes that building green buildings is an important and essential contribution that the construction industry can and should make towards achieving sustainability by envisioning the end result as a sustainable world.

4: Green Globes

Another international green building tool gaining popularity in the United States is the Green Globes™ green building assessment and rating system. The system is an outgrowth of Great Britain's BREEAM (Building Research Establishment's Environmental Assessment Method) building evaluation system. The BREEAM system for existing buildings was introduced in Canada in 1996. Initially called Green Leaf, the system evolved into an online evaluation system under the name Green Globes for Existing Buildings. By 2002, a new construction module had been developed that builds on and retains the same structure as the system previously established for existing buildings.

In 2004, the Green Building Initiative (GBI), a nonprofit educational organization headquartered in Portland, Oregon, acquired the promotional and marketing rights for the Green Globes tools in the United States. GBI's mission is to aid in the adoption of green building practices. Under GBI's aegis, Green Globes has been quick to gain momentum, competing effectively in the green building assessment market.

According to GBI, what differentiates Green Globes from other systems is its structure and assessment process. Green Globes was developed as an interactive Web-based tool, focused on providing guidance via a rating system designed to be a practical, flexible, and affordable alternative to other rating systems. GBI positions Green Globes as a simpler solution, one that, because it has been streamlined and simplified, not only provides all serious building professionals, practitioners, and interested parties with a tool for learning and implementing green building principles and practices but also enables those with minimal or no environmental background to use it successfully. Without any prior training and with only a computer with Internet access, a design team can be on the road to a green building rating in no time because the tool helps to quickly incorporate current and technically sound, sustainable design approaches to a building project.

The Green Globes assessment process has been enhanced with a web-enabled template giving a potential user a thirty-day trial. The user may then choose to subscribe and pay or let the trial expire. If the user lets the trial expire, all the data entered is saved for future use. Requests for third-party certification are also managed in the online template.

In addition to the different approach taken by the Green Globes structure, the market that GBI wants to serve is also somewhat different from that of USGBC. While both organizations address the general market of "mainstream builders, designers, and developers," GBI also reaches out specifically and directly to meet the needs of the residential market with the development of a tool in partnership with the National Association of Home Builders (discussed in the next chapter).

4.1 GBI Organization Overview

The country in which a project is located determines which organization will oversee application of the Green Globes  product. In Canada, the primary Green Globes product uses the brand name "Go Green Plus," now called BOMA BESt, and is operated by the Building Owners and Managers Association of Canada (BOMA Canada). In the United States, as mentioned previously, GBI holds the rights to the Green Globes product. GBI employs broad marketing strategies to engage all sectors and categories of stakeholders in the realm of building design, construction, operation, and various support roles and to successfully gain a share of the green building assessment market.

4.1.1 Membership Types, Levels, and Benefits

Becoming involved with GBI may appeal to a variety of industry professionals ranging from architects, builders, contractors, building owners and managers, manufacturers, vendors, trade associations, and utilities to service providers. GBI offers two different categories of membership (and three levels within each of those types) to meet the diverse needs of companies, organizations, and individuals interested in green building. As with all the systems and organizations covered in this book, rapid advancements in the industry require frequent updates to rating systems, membership structures, and any of a number of other issues, so be sure to check the GBI Web site for the most up-to-date information.

Commercial Memberships

The first category of commercial membership is Supporter. This category caters primarily to the needs and interests of manufacturers, trade associations, utilities, and service providers because this type of membership comes with an array of opportunities for the member to promote its services or wares to those interested in green building. Annual membership fees for Supporters are divided into three levels: bronze, silver, and gold. As you might expect, the number and type of benefits increase with each level from bronze to silver to gold, as does the annual membership fee.

The second type of commercial membership is the Voting Members category. Although the name "Member" might suggest otherwise, this category provides significant opportunities for companies and organizations that really want a deep level of involvement with GBI. The levels of this type of membership depend on the fee and entail a donation to GBI of $20,000, $50,000, and $100,000, respectively. Naturally, the more sizable the contribution is, the more substantial are the advantages that accompany it.

Student Affiliations

While there is no Student membership, GBI does offer students free access to the Green Globes New Construction tool for one project. Students can register for this access on the Web site. The student affiliation must be renewed each year the student is in school. Although the listing specifies that only one project can be registered under the student affiliation status, a phone number is given if additional school projects request the use of the tool.

Membership Benefits

Membership benefits vary based on the category and level of membership selected. Generally, however, the range of benefits that GBI offers includes various forms of visibility and recognition (e.g., in print, on the GBI Web site, at GBI events, and at trade shows) for a company or organization that plays a role in green building; educational resources and employee training programs; active participation in the direction that GBI takes and its leadership (e.g., through voting rights, committee seats, GBI board membership); complimentary use of the Green Globes New Construction tool; and complimentary third-party certification. However, those who just want to be involved on the periphery can simply become a "Friend of GBI" and receive the GBI email newsletter and other email campaigns by signing up on the Web site.

GBI for Home Builders

The Green Building Initiative provides multiple green building resources to home builder associations (HBAs) and builders across North America. Some of the offerings GBI provides include a comprehensive green building incentive database outlining federal, state, and local green building incentives; research reports; in-person and online interactive green building training; and marketing strategies and assistance to promote mainstream residential green building practices. The GBI supports local, HBA-driven green initiatives as well as the National Association of Home Builders (NAHB) National Green Building Program.

4.1.2 Organizational Structure

Like other nonprofits, GBI has a board of directors from the building industry, academia, nongovernmental organizations, construction companies, and architectural firms. The future goal of GBI is to have a thirty-seat board including ten representatives from each of the following categories: producers, users (construction trade, designers, engineers, etc.), and interested parties.

As opposed to the exponentially growing staff of USGBC (at least it seems exponential), daily GBI activities are overseen by a team of approximately fifteen staff members who handle the residential and commercial programming, marketing, educational sessions, software development, and administrative functions of the organization. This composition supports the organization's goals of being both affordable and Web-based.

GBI for Home Builders

The Green Building Initiative provides multiple green building resources to home builder associations (HBAs) and builders across North America. Some of the offerings GBI provides include a comprehensive green building incentive database outlining federal, state, and local green building incentives; research reports; in-person and online interactive green building training; and marketing strategies and assistance to promote mainstream residential green building practices. The GBI supports local, HBA-driven green initiatives as well as the National Association of Home Builders (NAHB) National Green Building Program.

4.2 Various Green Building Initiative Programs

GBI divides its software products into two categories: Commercial and Residential. This helps to keep the primary decisions simple for anyone and everyone interested in green building, whether or not they have a background in the industry and its methodologies. Within the online assessment tools, however, there are more options from which to choose. These are:

- Design of New Buildings or Significant Renovation
- Management and Operation of Existing Buildings
- Homes
- Building Energy Management (Canadian version only)
- Building Intelligence (Canadian version only)
- Fit-Up (Canadian version only)

While these look fairly similar to some of the categories covered by LEED, the Green Globes tools contain approximately half the number of options. Depending on your perspective, this simplification could be viewed as either good or bad; you decide based on your particular preference and experience. Given Green Globes's focus on simplicity, efficiency, and ease of use, the streamlining of the categories makes complete sense for their particular products.

4.2.1 Green Globes Rating System Overview

The Green Globes rating system, while definitely an assessment tool, attempts to emphasize guidance through the green building design and construction process. This is not a rating system you try to manage cross-sectionally through the process, looking at all the steps as the team moves forward. Instead, Green Globes is broken out very specifically into different stages of self-assessment through its established questionnaires, which in turn provide feedback to inform the next steps of the design process. The feedback comes in the form of reports and recommendations, including suggestions to think about as the design progresses.

GBI identifies eight different stages of development. The Green Globes rating system employs a cyclical process within those different stages of development, repeating similar steps over and over with slight shifts as the process moves forward. The approach is similar to a road circling a mountain to get up to the top; the team will hit all the cardinal directions (or in this case, green building strategies) a number of times (specifically eight) before reaching the top. Each time a strategy or concern is revisited, the project has moved a little farther along and the

vantage point of the strategy has shifted. It starts as a possibility being considered, then to a possibility being explored, to an element being integrated schematically, and finally to one being engineered to fit seamlessly into the design scheme. The moves are meant to be deliberate and repeated, allowing the design team to anticipate, research, and implement in a fluid process.

The first feedback loop with a system-generated assessment rating is a preliminary rating at the end of Schematic Design. At this stage, the online assessment guides the team toward the incorporation of elements such as energy modeling (through the EPA's Target Finder), life cycle cost analysis for various materials, and daylighting studies. The second feedback loop with an assessment rating occurs at the completion of construction documents, creating a conditional final self-assessment rating. The final step to achieving a Green Globes rating is to engage in a third-party onsite certification process after construction is completed.

The Green Globes rating system defines four levels a project can be awarded—from one to four Green Globes—depending on its achievements in going green. Of the 1,000 points available, the four tiers break down into the following categories:

- 35–54% (of 1,000 points) One Green Globe
- 55–69% Two Green Globes
- 70–84% Three Green Globes
- 85–100% Four Green Globes

4.2.2 The Stages of Assessment

The process begins with a system-generated assessment guided by Green Globes's detailed questionnaires. Following the preliminary assessment conducted at the end of Schematic Design, the Green Globes rating process continues with two distinct stages of third-party assessment. Stage 1 consists of a questionnaire-driven self-assessment completed based on the project's construction documents; Stage 2 entails a site visit conducted after construction is complete.

During Stage 1, the Green Globes assessor compares the questionnaire responses to the construction documents and other ancillary documentation submitted to demonstrate the alignment between the project's goals and the building's construction documents. As mentioned previously, a series of questions address each stage of the design process, followed by a series of next steps, which become more detailed with each successive stage. By filling out each section of the questionnaire in turn during the self-assessment process, the team and the client get a preliminary estimate of the overall greenness of the project as well as an indication of the overall score the project is likely to achieve. The project, however, does not receive an actual Green Globes rating until (1) the questionnaire responses in the Construction Documents stage have been completed; (2) the Stage 1 assessment is accomplished; and (3) the Stage 2 site visit takes place at the end of construction. The third-party assessment and certification process, if successful, results in a certified building and involves a fee. This ensures that the project actually meets the criteria that it claims to meet as indicated in the online questionnaire. This confirmation increases the credibility of the green building strategies employed, and the official rating entitles the building to a plaque and publicity.

4.3 Structure of the Guidelines

To maintain consistency and the ability to compare across the different guidelines contained in the system, I've chosen the Green Globes New Construction Module to illustrate the Green Globes process and guidelines in the discussion that follows.

4.3.1 Guideline Layout

In the Green Globes system, points are assigned based on a matrix of concerns that divides the process into both stages and sections. Each project has eight stages:

Stage 1: Predesign—Project Initial Questionnaire
Stage 2: Predesign—Site Analysis
Stage 3: Predesign—Programming
Stage 4: Schematic Design
Stage 5: Design Development
Stage 6: Construction Documents
Stage 7: Contracting and Construction
Stage 8: Commissioning

Additionally, there are seven sections that may apply to any given project:

Section 1: Project Management
Section 2: Site
Section 3: Energy
Section 4: Water
Section 5: Resources
Section 6: Emissions
Section 7: Indoor Environment

While most of the stages will use all seven sections, there are two exceptions. Stage 2, Predesign—Site Analysis, does not include questions regarding Project Management or Emissions because these are generally not part of predesign site analysis activities (and, if there happen to be a few, they can be covered elsewhere). Similarly, there is no Site Section in Stage 8 for Commissioning.

This cross-referencing of Stages and Sections is illustrated in an online, interactive matrix that GBI calls the Project Dashboard. The Dashboard, designed to show the current status of the project, illustrates those sections that have been completed and those aspects that still need attention from the project team. The boxes in the chart are color-coded to make it easy to see, at a glance, what has been started, what has not, and what is finished. Each of the matrix boxes symbolizes a series of questions that will ultimately determine the project's green designation and level. The number of questions in each section ranges from under ten to between thirty and forty, depending on the nature and depth of information required. The matrix is designed to be user-friendly. For example, when the cursor rolls over an individual box, the Dashboard displays the specific stage of development to which that particular questionnaire pertains. Online instructions are provided within the product to explain how the questionnaires are to be completed.

While the Project Dashboard is a powerful tool in application, as it is presented here it provides only a snapshot of cross-referenced categories in the matrix. To really understand them, it's useful to look more closely at each of the eight stages in the process, in the sequence in which they are meant to be used.

4.3.2 Stage 1: Pre-design—Project Initiation

The goal of Stage 1 is twofold: (1) to help teams think through issues that are likely to surface at some point during the design and construction process, and (2) to start the Integrated Design process. The questionnaire asks only for a "yes" or "no" response to different questions, and most of the issues raised in this section address intent. Because nothing has actually happened yet, many things can still be changed if necessary.

The first page of the questionnaire is simply a cover sheet that captures general building information, such as building type, gross floor area, and client information. A cover sheet

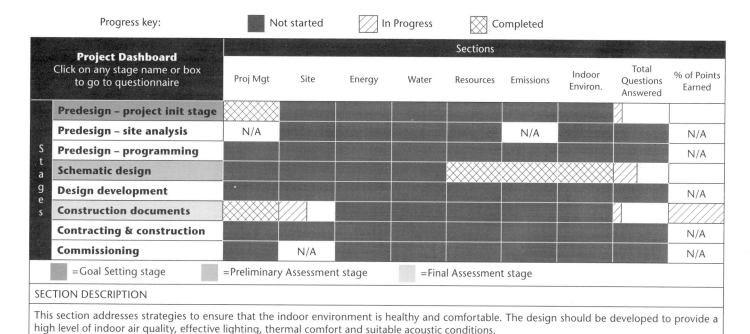

Progress key: ▮ Not started ◹ In Progress ⊠ Completed

Project Dashboard Click on any stage name or box to go to questionnaire	Sections								
	Proj Mgt	Site	Energy	Water	Resources	Emissions	Indoor Environ.	Total Questions Answered	% of Points Earned
Predesign – project init stage	⊠	▮	▮	▮	▮	▮	▮	◹	
Predesign – site analysis	N/A	▮	▮	▮	▮	N/A	▮	▮	N/A
Predesign – programming	▮	▮	▮	▮	▮	▮	▮	▮	N/A
Schematic design	▮	▮	▮	▮	⊠	⊠	⊠	◹	
Design development	▮	▮	▮	▮	▮	▮	▮	▮	N/A
Construction documents	⊠	◹	▮	▮	▮	▮	▮	◹	◹
Contracting & construction	▮	▮	▮	▮	▮	▮	▮	▮	N/A
Commissioning	▮	N/A	▮	▮	▮	▮	▮	▮	N/A

▮ =Goal Setting stage   ▮ =Preliminary Assessment stage   ▮ =Final Assessment stage

SECTION DESCRIPTION

This section addresses strategies to ensure that the indoor environment is healthy and comfortable. The design should be developed to provide a high level of indoor air quality, effective lighting, thermal comfort and suitable acoustic conditions.

Green Globes's Project Dashboard illustrates the stages and sections within the rating tool. Recreated with permission of GBI.

appears at the beginning of each of the stages included in the questionnaire. This is particularly helpful if a document is circulating among team members for individual input, or if there is more than one project following the Green Globe assessment guide at the same time in the office. Project Management, Policies and Practices is the first section of the questionnaire packet. Although there is no order specified for what must be completed when, if a team proceeds systematically through the Green Globes rating system as a project progresses, this will be the subject matter addressed first. The section uses

Yes/No questions to help the team think about its process and overarching goals for the project. Some typical questions are: *Are you using an integrated design process? Have you decided how long the building is going to be around? Has the team settled on a level of commissioning for the project?* By prodding the project management staff with these types of questions, Green Globes helps to clarify and emphasize the larger intentions of the design as envisioned by the management team.

In the later sections of Stage 1—such as Site, Energy, Water, and Resources—the questions tend to start with the phrase, "Is there a commitment . . . " Twenty-five of the last twenty-eight questions in this stage ask about the team's commitment. For example, *Is there a commitment to minimize the demand for potable water in the building and onsite?* And *Is there a commitment to avoid the use of ozone-depleting substances in the building?* Like the questions asked in the Project Management, Policies and Practices section, these questions help focus the design team on specific issues it will face as the project progresses. This approach also starts to speak directly to individual team members who are in charge of different aspects of the project, so that their direction and tasks may be a little clearer.

In addition to delineating specific commitments in this way, the larger objectives are also identified, subject by subject, within the sections. For example, the "Objective to provide a healthy environment for occupants" inside the Indoor Environment section includes the following two Yes/No questions: *Is there a commitment to provide healthy indoor air? Is there a commitment to control pollutants at source?* By giving a larger objective to the smaller, more precise goals, Green Globes tries to bridge the gap between project management and the beginning of technical implementation.

No supporting information is required during Stage 1, only the Yes/No responses to the questions. Because construction has not yet begun—and the drawing sets are in the very preliminary stages—these guiding questions, general in nature, seem to lead the team toward a green product.

4.3.3. Stage 2: Pre-design—Site Analysis

The Site Analysis stage has questions in only five of the seven sections, as noted previously. The intent of this stage is to find out what types of site possibilities have been taken into consideration during design. If the team is going through the checklist as suggested, probably not many drawings have been completed, and certainly no construction has started yet. The questions pertaining to site analysis are still exploratory, touching on those concerns that would, ideally, be addressed thus far in the design of a green building so that the team can assess how its project stacks up against those ideals at this early stage of the project.

There is no Project Management section in Stage 2, so the guidelines begin with actual site considerations for the project such as: site selection (e.g., use of brownfields, use of parklands, or project contributing to urban sprawl), night sky pollution (e.g., excessive artificial light making it difficult to see the stars in the sky at night), and an ecological assessment of the current flora and fauna. While these are not all of the topics covered, they give you an idea of what the rating system is looking for when it awards points. Again, the questions require only Yes/No responses.

The Energy section in the Site Analysis stage deals with internal and external energy required by the building. For example, the first question deals with the efficiency of the space, essentially asking if the building has been designed to be as small as possible and is not an overly designed behemoth of a building with excess space that needs to be conditioned. Feasibility studies of renewable energy strategies are also addressed, asking if each alternative has been evaluated. Regarding external aspects, the section asks about such things as the transportation energy that would be used to get to and from the site and whether there is nearby access to public transportation and/ or an alternative fueling station. The Water section of Stage 2 contains only three questions. Two of these questions can actually be answered "not applicable," so the design team may only have to deal with one question, which asks whether or not collecting rainwater is appropriate in the design. The other two questions deal with wastewater and greywater, inquiring about what local codes permit. For example, in many jurisdictions, greywater is not allowed for flushing toilets. Other local codes discourage or prohibit the use of greywater infiltration systems or living machines integrated into the landscape design. These two questions, however, ask if the design team has even looked at those possibilities as an option.

The Resources section is also small focusing primarily on the possibility of employing reused materials for construction. The first question addresses possible building reuse, while the second and third questions look at recycled materials and construction waste. Because, presumably, the design team has not yet gotten into the meat of the project, these initial stages are still very investigative and concentrate on possibilities to be considered for implementation. The possibilities are particularly useful for team members who are just getting into the design of green buildings because of the manner in which they lead the user through the thought process.

The final section of Stage 2 is Indoor Environment. A section of only four questions, it is intended to ensure that regional issues of mold and local issues of pollution, including radon and noise, have been explored. Additionally, the questions start to address the quality of the indoor environment by noting the importance of view corridors and connection to the natural environment.

Taken together, the first two sections of Green Globes help the project team address fundamental questions about the design and management process and also take the first step of site selection and analysis. While this approach may seem somewhat rudimentary to those who are highly experienced with green building, walking through these steps provides a kind of checklist for the team as a whole and a valuable resource for those just getting started.

4.3.4 Stage 3: Pre-design—Programming

Stage 3 is much bigger than those described thus far and, while Stage 3 is still on the front end of the entire construction process, the questions and issues addressed at this point are much more technical from the facilities perspective. The client contact in charge of facilities is likely to appreciate this increased level of detail as he or she gets involved in the programming details that are at the heart of Stage 3.

The section addressing Project Management and Policies consists of several parts. The first is Building Information, and it covers the requirements that have been put in place (probably written into the project specifications) to help achieve a green building. For example, this section asks, *Is there a requirement to purchase "green" products?* and *Is there a requirement that energy-efficient equipment be used?* These questions stretch the boundaries a little further than asking about the commitment to strategies, as in Stage 1, to whether these strategies are making it into the preliminary drawings and specifications. This is seen primarily in the questions that address the development of a Commissioning Brief, questions that basically outline how to write one. This section asks, *Does the document provide a Statement of Intent for each of the following systems . . . ?* and

then goes on to enumerate them (e.g., lighting control, refrigeration systems, water pumps, etc.).

The Site section looks at issues alluded to or suggested in previous stages, such as whether the site is contaminated (a brownfield) or is a wetland or wildlife corridor. This section also addresses "climatic and site features." A series of Yes/No questions deal with the team's attention to issues such as heat islands, sensitive topography, light pollution, site water management, and native ecology, and speak to the requirements that have been established for each.

The Energy section is where specific, quantitative targets begin to be set. The targets refer to specific standards such as ASHRAE 90.1-2004 and Energy Star Target Finder. These references help to solidify the intentions for the project by providing measurements to be used by the design team as it moves forward through the pre-design stage. However, the Energy section also asks the team to look at issues such as orientation on the site (with a preference for using topographic features for thermal benefit) as well as the benefits of using shading devices, window systems, and proper insulation. These issues can easily be identified at this stage and then translated into details and construction documents when the time comes. Identifying these issues before the team needs to think diligently about them is what makes this process most useful.

As seen previously in Stage 2, the Energy section also addresses energy that would be expended getting to and from the building, as well as in support of those transportation methods. This is where references to such enhancements as changing rooms for a certain portion of the population to encourage biking or walking to work will be found, as well as questions about carpool parking and alternative fueling stations in close proximity. There is even a question about what "close proximity" actually means, but that will be addressed in Stage 6.

Quantifiable intents are also contained in the Water section; there, they are intended to examine how different types of buildings are likely to provide different types of water savings. Again, this is a great strategy for guiding design as the team proceeds, especially if they are not, at the outset, familiar with water-saving strategies. For example, one of the major questions of this section asks what type of water conservation has been targeted for the building type. An office, for instance, may have its target use set at less than 35 gal/sf/yr, less than 20 gal/sf/yr, or less than 10 gal/sf/yr. These targets provide a good idea of what the design team should be considering as it prepares to start the official design stages. Other areas addressed by the Stage 3 Water section include the amount of potable water consumed by interior plumbing fixtures, the use of water in cooling towers, water necessary for irrigation, and, finally, the treatment of greywater from the building itself.

The Stage 3 Resources section also addresses several key issues regarding the use of natural resources. The first entails a sweeping question about the life cycle impact of materials, essentially asking if there are systems or materials the team plans on using in the building that should be looked at for their possible environmental strain and/or embodied energy. While at this stage the question can be answered with a simple "yes" or "no," the question is nevertheless a complex one that requires serious consideration—and one that ultimately requires documentation when the time comes for validation. Other, slightly more straightforward questions concern reused and locally available materials, the reuse of existing buildings, and whether or not the design incorporates qualities such as durability, adaptability, and disassembly.

While durability, adaptability, and disassembly are very important concepts in the philosophy of sustainable design, they are more difficult to quantify. Other guidelines and rating systems do not address these qualities directly, and Green Globes is to be commended for incorporating these more abstract concepts pertinent to the changing construction industry. These concepts do, of course, apply to the more measurable issues such as maintenance where concerns such as durability and lifecycle may be inferred, even when they are not overtly addressed.

The Resources Section also addresses topics such as the inclusion of the recycling of construction waste in a construction management plan, as well as facilities for recycling. Going beyond the recycling criteria contained in some guidelines,

Green Globes asks if it is appropriate to compost in the building and if that has been accommodated.

The Emissions Effluents and Other Impacts section throws a sweeping net over the issue of pollution—both that which comes from the greater building systems as well as emissions that may affect the interior of the building. The concerns regarding emissions leaving the building include air emissions, ozone depleting substances such as refrigeration components, wastewater effluents, and even fuel storage tanks if they are necessary to the program. Interior to the building, emissions issues include the use of asbestos, radon, and PCBs, as well as any hazardous materials that may be required for use onsite. Bridging the indoor and outdoor realms is the topic of pest control and how those annoyances may be managed, with or without chemicals.

The last stage of Pre-Design is Indoor Environment, which again encapsulates all aspects of the indoor environment from pollution to thermal strategies and on to daylighting and views. The primary goal of this section is to ensure that issues concerning ventilation, filtration, and indoor air pollutants are clearly on the design team's radar screen. Additionally, this section addresses the larger concepts of daylighting, thermal comfort, and acoustics, which incorporate smaller details such as avoiding glare, adhering to ASHRAE Standard 55-2004, and providing sound attenuation. These are all things that the design team should be thinking about as it moves forward.

Questions such as *Are there lighting requirements that glare be avoided?* prompt the team to do so.

Keep in mind that these guidelines are still addressing the pre-design phase and therefore are reminders rather than requirements set in stone.

4.3.5 Stage 4: Schematic Design

As Stage 4 commences, the project team is likely to be putting pen to paper. It is at this point when specific ideas begin to bubble up and are discussed by the team for their appropriateness, feasibility, and cost. All of the suggestions made thus far are about to get hardlined into documents that will become the approved specifications and construction documents.

The Project Management section of Stage 4 is fairly simple. It asks that the team implement an integrated design process, one that brings every member of the design team around the table. Ideally, this will produce a holistic design, one that addresses sustainability in each facet of the project and works on creating synergies across the board. Even so, these integrated design questions remain fairly general. For instance, one question asks: *Does the design process use a team approach?* Depending on how the team currently works, the answer might be a simple and straightforward "yes," or the design process might need to be molded to fit the established team process.

Other Project Management topics include looking at environmental purchasing and the creation of a commissioning plan. The statements ask about the preparation of a "Conceptual Design Report" but do not outline exactly what that report should entail or require. That is left up to the project management team.

The Site section in Stage 4 looks slightly more in-depth than in the previous section addressing site considerations. Section 4 asks basic questions about what site surveys are being applied and how the site has been categorized or zoned. Section 4 also suggests strategies for addressing the ecological impact of the site, indicating yet-unnamed tactics to reduce the heat island effect or the use of native vegetation onsite. There is also a suggestion to address the ecology of the site by either remediating a contaminated site or by building on currently existing natural features of the site.

The Energy section of Stage 4 is substantial, getting into some of the more difficult topics regarding the engineering of the building. Although long, the Energy section is still fairly general. It addresses issues such as the establishment of an energy target through simulation software and the optimization of space efficiency in the plan. Essentially, the questions are concerned with whether or not the building has been downsized as much as possible. Form-giving features that would impact energy usage are addressed here, including passive solar gains, thermal loss, and natural ventilation. The issue of daylighting also makes an appearance in this section.

In previous stages, daylighting was relegated to the Indoor Environment section. This is one instance in which a specific design strategy is split up among different sections, depending on the impact or facet of the strategy being addressed. Here, daylighting questions refer to the penetration depth, glazing selections, building orientation, shading strategies, and lighting controls and how each of these might affect the energy consumption of the building.

The Energy section also contains questions regarding the selection of materials for the building envelope, implementation of a continuous air barrier, and other issues that easily translate into construction details. Energy metering is also addressed, as are items deemed energy-efficient systems. These include elements such as high-efficiency lamps, task lighting, heat pumps, building automation systems, and other systems that would lighten the collective energy load.

The final batch of concerns integrated into the Energy section looks at the incorporation of renewable energy sources into the design, as well as the transportation energy consumed in getting to and from the building. These are fairly close repeats to the issues seen in previous sections, but are phrased in a slightly more concrete way. While Stage 3 asked, *Is there an indication of the percentage of renewable energy (from grid and/ or onsite sources) that should be integrated?*, Stage 4 asks, *Are the following renewable energy systems being considered?* This allows for the selection of active solar-heating, high-efficiency, low-emission biomass combustion, wind energy, etc. The questions are still suggestive, and slightly repetitive.

Water section topics are very similar to those found in the previous stage; the change, essentially, is that some strategies get more specific. For example, the guidelines start to ask about specific types of water features rather than simply gallons of water saved (although those are addressed as well). Additional water-saving strategies are also called out, such as desiccant cooling systems (an evaporative cooling strategy using a desiccant to attract water molecules and dehumidify the air) and xeriscaping (landscaping that allows the reduction or elimination of additional irrigation). Other strategies, such as those addressing onsite greywater treatment, are phrased nearly the same as in previous stages.

The Resources section also addresses the same overall topics as previously, but looks at them from a different perspective. General areas of interest include the environmental impact of materials and systems, the use of non-renewable resources, building reuse, and those new concerns of durability, adaptability, and disassembly. When addressing the environmental impact of materials, the guidelines now start to call out specific building assemblies such as foundation and floor materials, roof assemblies, and structural systems. This helps to break down the area of concern into manageable parts rather than lumping all materials in the building into one category. As with previous sections, some of the questions seem to repeat, such as those referring to facilities for recycling and composting. For example, Stage 3 asked, *Is there a requirement for provision of separate waste separation, storage, and handling facilities for consumer recyclables such as used paper, newspaper, newsprint, cardboard, glass, metal, and plastic?* Stage 4 now asks, *Will there be facilities for future occupants to handle and store consumer recyclables?* These are notably similar and are intended to take the design team through the rudimentary steps of creating a solid green building product.

Likewise, the Stage 4 Emissions section takes a more focused tone regarding topics raised in Stage 3. In Stage 4, for example, "emissions" does not specifically address pollution into the atmosphere. Rather, it tackles not only air pollutants but also chemicals contributing to ozone depletion, sewer contamination, and pest management strategies. There is also a small section addressing hazardous material treatment, if that is going to be a necessary evil in the project. The phrasing in Stage 4 is different, switching from *Is there a requirement to create conditions for the application of integrated pest management?* in Stage 3 to Stage 4 where the question becomes *Will there be design features that promote integrated pest management?*

Three pages of Stage 4 questions are devoted to Indoor Environment, tackling topics such as effective ventilation, indoor pollutants, daylighting, actual lighting design, thermal comfort strategies, and acoustic comfort. Indicators of actual measurements that should be targeted show up here—for example, accordance with ventilation rates stated by ASHRAE

62-2004 or CO_2 levels not exceeding 800 parts per million. However, watery generalities, such as *Will there be easy access for cleaning and inspecting air filters?* still abound.

Questions and intentions begin to solidify through the last half of the established stages. As noted, there are not a lot of differences thus far between stages. For ease of comprehension and also to avoid repetition, the descriptions that follow concentrate only on new additions to stages or sections and differences in phrasing and emphasis between stages.

4.3.6 Stage 5: Design Development

In Stage 5, ideas that have been with the project since they were mere inklings in the minds of design team members are now being thought through in more detail. Many ideas are reaching the make-it-or-break-it point; some may never be heard from again (or, at least, not until the next project).

The Stage 5 Project Management section is now down to five questions from the seven in Stage 4. The first three questions address the integrated design process and are essentially the same as Stage 4. The last three questions in Stage 4, referring to different parts of the commissioning plan documentation, are combined into one question in Stage 5. It asks, *Is documentation being prepared to support comprehensive, best practice commissioning?* Not much here has changed, barely even the phrasing. The fifth question addresses the incorporation of an environmental purchasing plan for energy-efficient equipment, which is a pol-

icy decision that will need to be addressed by staff, but can be broached by the project team. As the design team moves on to the Site section of Stage 5, the questions are geared toward tracking progress in achieving the project's stated intentions. While most hard numbers and quantifiable aspects for what exactly will make the final project green are still not required at this point, there are distinct nudges that continue to urge the design team in that direction. Because the various stages are specific and deliberate, they make the process both obvious and transparent, guiding the team, step by step, linking and sequencing the various activities to help ensure continuity as the project moves forward. For example, in Stage 4, the team is asked if the site analysis conducted previously has been implemented. For some teams, the question may feel repetitive of earlier stages and their response may well be "Yes, of course!" For others, however, the question may serve as a useful reminder to follow through on that detail.

Because energy is one of the more hard-hitting aspects of green building design, the Energy section questions tend to focus on quantifiable factors. For example, one of the questions asks specifically for the energy efficiency of the building as indicated by the energy model. Other questions regarding energy efficiency—such as questions that pertain to how considerations such as topography and microclimate are factored into design development—are phrased slightly differently from one stage to the next, reflecting the project's progress.

The fundamental shift that occurs between Stage 4 and Stage 5 in the Green Globes system is from questions that ask if strategies are being considered to questions that ask if strategies are being applied. While only one or two words may have changed in the phrasing, these are significant words and the resulting questions are very different. Instead of asking *if* the team is committed to an approach (theoretically), the question becomes *has it* committed to the approach. This is where some solidification in the measure finally begins to appear. There are still no supporting documents for clarification, nor are there yet requirements for any proof as the design team checks the appropriate boxes, but the slight shift indicating that actual implementation is occurring is now present in the shape of the questions. The balance of the Energy section, as well as the Water, Resources, Emissions, and Indoor Environment sections, continue in the same vein.

4.3.7 Stage 6: Construction Documents (Plans and Specifications)

Stage 6 is the longest stage of the Green Globes rating system. It represents the culmination of the planning process, the point at which, as anyone who has experienced the building and construction process knows, the rubber hits the road. There is a huge amount of information to gather as design ideas become construction documents and details and the specification book for the project gets assembled. Questions in Stage 6 shift in phrasing to the past tense. Hence, the question that previously was *Does the design process use a team approach?* is now *Was a team approach used during the design process?* By the time the team reaches this point, there is no going back to redo what has already been done.

Similarly, to make sure no one is fibbing on their questionnaires, "Prove It" questions begin to appear. For example, questions such as the following predominate: *Have aspects of green product specifications been incorporated? Give examples of specified products reflecting green specifications.* Not only does the team have to click on the "Yes" box, it must also cite actual examples of the green products incorporated into the design.

The Project Management section of Stage 6 adds the new first category not included in previous stages: the Emergency Response Plan. It addresses whether or not the project's environmental goals and procedures are incorporated into the emergency response plan. Similarly, the area of Commissioning Plan—Documentation gets into more detail. The guidelines address whether specific commissioning steps have been incorporated. For example, one possible response statement is: *A Commissioning Authority has been engaged.*

The second section, addressing Site, also gets into more specifics. It asks about the exact type of site being used. Is it an existing serviced site, one that has been remediated, or a new, greenfield site? This is one step beyond the level of inquiry in the last phase that was still vague, asking simply if site analysis had been applied to the site plan. In Stage 6, however, specific measurements have been defined, referring to site considerations including floodplains, wetlands, and wildlife corridors.

Questions regarding ecological impact also get more detailed. Specific measurements to which the project will adhere are expected to be provided in the responses. For example: *At least 35 percent of all impervious surfaces will be shaded, preferably with vegetation as opposed to built elements such as terraces, shading elements, or trellis*. Additional measurements are also noted, such as measurements for reflectance on high-albedo roofs and the portion of the roofs that will be covered (75 percent). The guidelines even address the flight paths of birds, and ask that the design reduce the frequency of birds colliding with the building. This type of suggestion helps address larger aspects of sustainability, beyond what is seen in some of the other green building guidelines. A similar level of detail is present in the questions pertaining to watershed features and site ecology.

The Energy section of Stage 6 requests details that indicate a level of completion and rigor that should be seen at this stage in the project. Now, not only do the questions ask about the energy saved, but also the value of the carbon dioxide emissions savings—an actual, calculated percentage, and not just a Yes/No response. Like the previous sections described in this stage, the Energy section also seeks validation through questions that now expect responses describing how the design accomplished the strategies identified during the earlier stages.

To avoid repeating the phrasing or specific intentions of questions in the remaining sections of Stage 6, suffice it to say that the progression of the Water and Resources sections are very similar to those just described. Questions are phrased in the past tense, asking about what has been done specifically rather than about intention. The Resources section asks for details regarding the types of materials to be used, assemblies, and life-cycle assessments, but it does not get into such specifics as what "durability" is or what quantities of recycled materials are targeted.

The Construction Documents stage, with the Conditional Final Rating, is the principal stage used by the Green Globes assessor to perform the Stage I and II assessment protocols. The remaining sections continue to document project activity and are always recommended. However, the assessment process culminates here with its checks and balances on whether the Green Globes responses were implemented.

4.3.8 Stage 7: Contracting and Construction

At this stage, all of the design team's intentions have been noted, clarified, and included in the construction documents and specification booklets. All that is left is to implement. Rather than looking at the details of the building's design and possible green building strategies, Stage 7 focuses on what is happening on the construction site.

Stage 7 guidelines comprise only eight pages (less than half the length of the Construction Documents stage), and one of those eight pages is the building information cover sheet.

The sections average just three questions each, the exception being the Project Management section, with nine questions.

The Project Management section of Stage 7 explores the details of the construction process, including how subcontractors are being trained and how the process is monitored on the construction site. The bulk of this section asks if the contractors and subcontractors are using the same environmentally friendly philosophies in the construction process as those that were incorporated into the building design. For example, are the contractors using energy-efficient lighting onsite? Are renewable resources being used to create energy for construction practices? Is there a demolition waste management/reduction work plan? Finally, there is a section at the end of Stage 7 that looks at disturbance and other negative effects (such as airborne particles and noise) that the construction activities are causing to neighbors of the project.

4.3.9 Stage 8: Commissioning

The home stretch—the final stage of Green Globes —is Commissioning. By now the building construction is complete and the team is getting down to the nitty-gritty. This questionnaire is only three pages long and focuses primarily on testing all the systems installed in the building. The Project Management section deals with certificates being signed off (Certificate of Occupancy) and whether training has been provided to those users of the building who will actually be operating and managing the sys-

tems installed. All of the design team's good intentions could go to waste if the systems are not operated properly. For that reason alone, it is very important in nearly all green buildings that training be supplied for those who will be handling the systems.

The remainder of the Commissioning stage checklist deals with checking the various systems. Questions at this final stage include, *Has the building envelope been commissioned for air leakage? Have mechanical systems to recycle or separate waste been commissioned?* These are Yes/No questions, and none of them really addresses the findings of the commissioning, with the exception of the question addressing the Energy Target, which asks, *Are energy performance targets being met?* This question goes to the heart of green building design: Are the intentions of the design, so long in planning, producing the desired results?

4.4 Discussions About Green Globes

An obvious question exists regarding the validity of simply checking boxes as a design team proceeds through a project. It does not take too much imagination to envision some situations in which project teams might be tempted to shuffle answers to favor a more positive green building outcome. Not everyone is as trustworthy as we would like to think. And who would really know if it were simply a matter of checking boxes to achieve a green rating?

GBI's response to this concern is the two-stage, third-party assessment process. Note also that some data sets are required with submission, in addition to complete design documentation including plans, specifications, energy simulation and target finder results, meeting notes, life cycle assessment documentation (LCA), lighting levels, and so forth.

Another question about Green Globes centers on its emphasis on simplification of the assessment tool. Of course it is easier for beginners to understand the basic, simplified questions in Stages 1 and 2. However, the simplified questions seen specifically in Stages 1 and 2 of the system are also fairly general. They require no supporting documentation for feeling out gray areas (which are inevitable in something as complex as green building). While documentation is required for different credits at later stages in the process, many of the initial simplified credits in Stage 1 and Stage 2 carry as much weight as the more technical elements of the later stages, but without substantial support. Some guidance is provided, however, in the form of tool tips, reports, etc. These are designed to help project teams better understand the applicable criteria.

For example, one of the questions found in Stage 1 asks, *Is there a commitment to provide facilities that will help to minimize the amount of waste generated during building occupancy?* If we were to break down this question, a number of other questions would emerge, such as: To what extent are we to minimize waste? Does that mean zero waste? Some other number? How do we know what the waste was to begin with so that we can minimize it? Also, what kind of waste are we talking about? Paper waste?

Compostable waste? Wastewater? If we can divert that waste to somewhere else, does it still count as waste, as in the instance of organic material that can be composted? While this is a relatively straightforward breakdown of one of the simple questions in Stage 1, you get the idea how a team might move beyond simplistic thinking to more complex and more technologically sophisticated and nuanced thinking by the prompts and avenues for exploration of the Green Globes process of inquiry.

The initial fuzziness dissipates as the program advances through its various stages. By Stage 3, there are more concrete indications of what would and would not qualify as green. For example, one question asks, *Is there a requirement that at least 75 percent of all plant species planted on the site should be native to the local area?* That statement is both easily understood and quantified. There are, however, still some questions that might cause confusion, such as: *Is there a requirement to optimize the space efficiency of the building?* Efficient space by one person's standards may be entirely different from what is acceptable to another. Green Globes provides no clarification about what this means and no suggested measure for quantifying the intent.

That raises an issue regarding the value of intent in this method of assessment. As we have seen, the first four stages and portions of the fifth stage ask solely about the intent and process of the design. An argument could be made as to whether this even matters. As an analogy, should I get points for simply *thinking* about helping an elderly person across the street, or only if I actually do it? If we are talking about issues that have a heavy impact on important topics such as climate change, land use, water use, and resource scarcity, is there room for giving credit to intentions? That could be debated.

The concerns above are mitigated somewhat by the high level of competency of the Green Globe third-party assessors. In addition, the flexibility of the system allows for partial credit for any question, if that is all the project merits on a particular issue. This partial credit, and the fact that the system is rated on a 1,000-point scale, enables the project's score to be fine-tuned and arguably more accurate. Also, Green Globes has incorporated life-cycle assessment into their system as outlined by the Athena Institute (reviewed in a sidebar in Chapter 5) to provide additional rigor.

It is important to note that the Green Globes tool has been shepherded through the American National Standards Institute (ANSI) standard certification process since 2006, and the second public comment period for the latest revision was completed in December 2008. A new Green Globes standard to be rolled out in mid-2009, Green Globes v.2 American Green Building Standard, addressing many of the issues discussed above. It is considerably more detailed and rigorous, while still retaining the foundational Green Globes structure and processes. Since ANSI third-party review was still under way when this book went to press, very little information was available yet for inclusion here regarding the new Green Globes standard.

The new version of Green Globes for New Construction will incorporate some new and updated criteria, the most significant of which involve energy performance, carbon emissions, and Life Cycle Assessment. The Energy Performance criteria will allow for alternate paths to determine the design energy consumption—a prescriptive approach for small buildings, and simulation/benchmarking approach for larger commercial buildings. The determination of carbon emissions will be strengthened in the 2009 version, through an analysis in the energy performance section, and an increased emphasis of LCA, which addresses construction materials' total environmental footprint from cradle to grave. The Green Globes LCA calculator will be integrated into the tool, as well as a Water Conservation calculator. Despite the increased intensity of the new ANSI certified Green Globes tool, the built-in efficiency of utilizing web-enabled, interactive green building assessment will be maintained.

The Green Globes v.2 American Green Building Standard to be issued in mid-2009 is, as of the writing of this book, on its way to becoming the second ANSI-certified green building standard in the United States beyond NAHBGreen. LEED, because of the many versions of its rating system (EB, CI, Homes, ND, NC, etc.), has not been put through the ANSI certification process. USGBC is, however, an ANSI certified standards developer. Value exists in each of these options: using a standard that is ANSI certified or using standards promulgated by an ANSI certified standards developer.

Officially launched in February 2008 by the National Association of Home Builders (NAHB), the National Green Building Program™, or NAHBGreen™, is another green building rating system gaining a stronghold in the construction market. Many in mainstream home building have perceived LEED for Homes certification to be relatively costly and also to cater to boutique firms producing high-end homes. By contrast, NAHBGreen was designed to suit the needs of mainstream homebuilders and developers as well as advanced green custom home builders. NAHB's members account for more than 80 percent of American-built homes each year. The current NAHB rating systems are similar to Green Globes in its positioning as a more affordable, simplified process. There are two green rating systems published by NAHB: the *Model Green Home Building Guidelines*, first published in 2005; and the *ICC-700 National Green Building Standard*, which has been officially approved by the American National Standards Institute (ANSI.) These two rating systems, supported by the larger NAHBGreen program, are structured to encourage the design and construction of green homes that are geographically, climatically, and economically appropriate. The program also strives for a more streamlined process to certify homes under the larger NAHBGreen program in an effort to meet the needs of a wider range of builders and consumers; from small mom-and-pop companies to larger, nationally known home builders.

Don't be confused: local home builders associations (HBAs) have used the NAHB Model Green Home Building Guidelines for some time. These fundamental guidelines have been the basis on which many local HBAs developed their own green scoring criteria and certifications in versions specific to their particular region. As a result, today there are many viable, locally focused green programs and home certifications offered around the country.

Published in early 2009, the *ICC-700 National Green Building*

Standard was developed in a partnership between NAHB and the International Code Council (ICC). A nationally-recognized consensus approach that was developed by ANSI was used to create the rating system. The Standard is unique in that it is applicable to both new construction and renovations, as well as single-family homes, multi-family structures, and green residential developments.

While NAHBGreen is administered by the national NAHB organization, local HBAs and other programs are given the option to affiliate with the national NAHBGreen program. This allows these smaller groups to share in the marketing and advocacy tools that have been developed at the national level and participate in a consistent program across the country. One goal of NAHBGreen is to provide the opportunity for every local HBA—some 800+ of them—to adapt, administer, and oversee their own green education and advocacy initiatives while having access to a consistent and nationally recognized certification process. While the option remains for an HBA to develop a local rating system and certification, NAHBGreen provides a convenient and cost-effective alternative while providing local HBAs with access to nationally developed education and marketing tools. In most areas builders and their customers seeking NAHBGreen certification may choose whether to use the Model Green Homebuilding Guidelines or the National Green Building Standard when designing, building and certifying a home.

NAHBGreen, much like USGBC's LEED system, requires third-party verification to certify a green building in the program, regardless of whether the Guidelines or the Standard is used. LEED uses a combination of prescriptive and performance-based strategies to cater to a professional population in commercial architecture that has, for a few years now, been formally introduced to and potentially interested in green building strategies. Similarly, green home building has been going on for years (the NAHB's annual green building conference marks its eleventh year in 2009) but green homes have only recently hit the homeowners' wavelength, as well as market-savvy homebuilders. This group is now taking a real interest in green building, especially with the Obama administration's emphasis on weatherization. The tools that NAHB has put together were created with this group in mind as well as green building veterans.

The flexibility inherent in the NAHB rating systems and the simplified certification system is focused on easing the transition for homebuilders going green, without compromising the rigor needed to encourage market change. To this end, both NAHB rating systems incorporate a unique scoring structure. Projects that are seeking certification through either the Guidelines or the Standard must satisfy baseline criteria as defined by each rating tool in each of the different areas of green building. These criteria thresholds increase as builders seek higher certification levels. As part of the certification, in addition to the required baseline points, the projects must also accrue a certain number of additional points in any area of the builder's choosing. This additional level of flexibility allows the builder to make specific choices to ensure the final building is both market- and climate-appropriate; for example, builders in dry climates can emphasize water efficient features while those in colder areas can focus on the building envelope and efficient heating systems. Either way, each home can be recognized and certified as appropriate for the given conditions.

5.1 Organization Overview

You can think of NAHB as the voice of America's housing industry. In this guise, NAHB addresses concerns of home builders and homeowners alike. A trade association, the NAHB has more than 800 local groups throughout the United States. NAHB's headquarters in Washington, DC, employs more than 300 people. The organization's mission (as articulated in its literature and on its Web site) focuses on the following goals:

- Balanced national legislative, regulatory, and judicial public policy.
- Public appreciation for the importance of housing and those who provide it.
- The premier resource for industry information, education, research, and technical expertise.

Threshold Point Ratings for Green Building				
Performance Level Points [1,2]				
Green Building Categories	Bronze	Silver	Gold	Emerald
Lot Design, Preparation, and Development	39	66	93	119
Resource Efficiency	45	79	113	146
Energy Efficiency	30	60	100	120
Water Efficiency	14	26	41	60
Indoor Environmental Quality	36	65	100	140
Operation, Maintenance, and Buildingowner Education	8	10	11	12
Additional Points from any category	222	406	558	697

[1] In addition to the threshold number of points in each category, all mandatory provisions of ech category shall be implemented.

[2] For dwelling units greater than 4,000 square feet (372 square meters), the number of points in Category 7 (Additional Points from any category) shall be increased in accordance with Section 601.1 of the standard. The "Total Points" shall be increased by the same number of points.

Point thresholds for the four different levels of green building certification as outlined by NAHB's standard. Recreated courtesy of NAHB.

- Improved business performance of its members and affiliates.
- Effective management of staff, financial, and physical resources to satisfy the association's needs.

Their vision is to "create an environment in which:

- All Americans have access to the housing of their choice and the opportunity to realize the American dream of homeownership.
- Builders have the freedom to operate as entrepreneurs in an open and competitive environment.
- Housing and those who provide it are recognized as the strength of the nation."

These statements constitute the fuel that drives NAHB's efforts on behalf of its members, shaping a climate in which all NAHB members can be competitive and successful in the home building industry and be recognized as a force in the American economy. As the general public's awareness surrounding energy consumption, water usage, and the environment in general increased and other organizations with green building rating systems began to incorporate the residential sector into their systems, the NAHB recognized—and responded to—the needs of its home builder members for green building strategies tailored to that construction industry niche.

5.1.1 Membership Levels

The membership structure in the NAHB is almost the reverse of that used by USGBC. Prospective members of NAHB (whether individuals or companies/organizations) join the local HBA and thus gain access to other levels of the organization. For example, in Durham, North Carolina, a member would join the Durham, Orange & Chatham County HBA and as a result of that membership have access to the state organization (North Carolina Home Builders Association) and the National Association of Home Builders (NAHB)—all for the price of membership at the local level. USGBC, on the other hand, requires a firm or organization to join nationally, and individuals to join locally.

Several levels of membership are available to individuals within the local HBAs although the specific levels may vary depending on location and an area's population and needs. Continuing with the example of Durham, the Durham, Orange & Chatham County HBA has three different levels at which an individual can join, provided that the person meets the qualifications for membership in one of the defined categories: Builder, Associate, or Affiliate. The Builder category accepts those with experience in building who either hold a general contractor's license themselves or represent a firm that holds such a license. The Associate category is for those who are not necessarily doing the building per se, but who are employed or engaged by the industry and profession. This would include the trades—plumbers, electricians, masons, etc. The third category, Affiliates, includes project managers, administrative support, and other similar professionals within an HBA member company.

This membership structure is less complex than that of either the USGBC or Green Globes. The structure caters primarily to those on the ground who are working with specific local groups rather than to organizations that want to be involved at the national level. This allows for local modification not only for the organizations themselves but also for the standards that are put in place.

5.1.2 Organizational Structure

As a trade association, the NAHB is member-driven and focuses on supporting the needs of its members in the home building construction industry. NAHB has more than 200,000 members around the country. The individual state and local associations are arranged into state-specific groups; individuals from these state groups are elected to the NAHB's board of directors. As is true of USGBC and the Green Building Initiative, the NAHB has an all-volunteer board—a choice intended to maintain the integrity of the organization and its progress. Next in line in the top ranks of the NAHB's volunteer leadership are its senior officers: the president, first vice president, vice president/treasurer (one seat), vice president/secretary (one seat), and the immediate past president. These individuals are elected by the board of directors at the NAHB's annual meeting.

The national vice presidents (also elected by the board of directors) are arranged in a regional structure, with the country broken out into fifteen areas. The national vice presidents work closely with the senior officers to ensure strong communication between the local/regional and national levels of the organization. Follow the "NAHB Leadership" link on the organization's Web site to find a breakdown of the areas and the contact information for the national vice president responsible for your area.

Within this structure, a number of substructures exist to help members get the most out of their involvement. One example of this is the NAHB's use of "councils," or special interest groups. These councils include:

- Building Systems Councils (groups such as the Log Homes Council, Modular Building Systems Council, and the Concrete Home Building Council, among others)
- Commercial Builders Council
- Multifamily
- National Sales and Marketing Council
- NAHB Remodelers Council
- 50+ Housing Council
- Women's Council

These groups allow those with common interests to interact at a deeper level and be better served by the association.

> **The Athena Institute:** (www.athenasmi.org) The Athena Institute is a nonprofit organization that provides assessment tools to the building industry to help meet builders' targeted sustainability goals. The institute's two primary software tools are the ATHENA® Impact Estimator for Buildings, which looks at whole buildings and assemblies in terms of life-cycle assessment (LCA) methods, and the ATHENA® EcoCalculator for Assemblies, which calculates instant LCA information for typical building assemblies based on the information entered into the tool. The organization also provides LCA databases, consulting services for building assessment and training, and general sustainability guidance through the maze of information available in the marketplace. The Institute has its headquarters in Ontario, Canada, and has a U.S. office in Kutztown, Pennsylvania.

5.2 NAHBGreen Scoring Systems Overview

The overarching NAHBGreen framework supports two rating systems; the *NAHB Model Green Home Building Guidelines* and the ANSI approved *National Green Building Standard*. In addition to new, single and multi-family homes, land development projects and residential remodeling projects can also be certified in the NAHBGreen program using the National Green Building Standard as the rating system. The *NAHB Model Green Home Building Guidelines* can only be applied to new, single-family homes.

The NAHB Model Green Home Building Guidelines were created through a collaborative process, engaging members (from all three membership categories), shareholders, and homeowners. The development process looked first at existing local green home programs, some of which are described in Chapter 6, Local Green Building Guidelines. These programs were primarily those created by local HBAs, but also included some nonprofit programs as well as some established by the public sector. Secondly, the association reviewed all NAHB-endorsed energy efficiency programs. Then the group reviewed prominent life-cycle analysis tools known in the United States and Canada, primarily tools developed by Building for Environmental and Economic Sustainability (BEES, described in Chapter 2) and the Athena Institute. ATHENA® is the life-cycle assessment system that Green Globes has incorporated into its rating system.

Once the task force in charge of conducting the research for the National Standard initiative agreed on the list of items and criteria to be included, it looked at each credit from three different perspectives: (1) environmental impact, (2) building science and best building practices, and (3) ease of implementation. These factors were not given equal weight. Instead, they were weighted in the order that they have been listed here, with environmental impact being the most important and ease of implementation the least. Additional details regarding these three factors can be found within the guideline document.

While both the *NAHB Model Green Home Building Guidelines*

and the *ICC 700-2008 National Green Building Standard* were created through a collaborative processes, as of writing this book, the National Green Building Standard is the only green building rating system to have been approved by ANSI. The pedigree offers users the assurance that the system was created by a qualified and diverse group of industry participants and that public input was given full consideration. In addition to builders, the consensus committee for the National Green Building Standard included representatives from the U.S. Department of Energy, the Environmental Protection Agency, the U.S. Green Building Council, building code officials, energy efficiency experts, relevant product associations, and representatives from regional green building programs. The process also included two periods of public comment on two working drafts before being considered for ANSI approval. A commentary piece to the National Green Building Standard, in development at the time of writing, will expand on the intent of the items within it, expounding on the intent and reasoning behind each line item in the standard, as well as additional resources, etc. The standard itself is primarily the rating system, rules for compliance, and only a few dozen definitions and resources. The rating system includes mandatory and discretionary items addressing lot and site development, resource efficiency, energy efficiency, water efficiency, indoor environmental quality, and the operation, maintenance, and owner education of the building's systems.

One interesting aspect of the NAHB's National Green Build-ing Standard is the location/region it chose as the basis for its Standard. The NAHB decided to use a hypothetical building in Baltimore, Maryland, a location that fits into Zone 4 of the U.S. Department of Energy's established climate zone map. Design considerations for this hypothetical home form the basis for the Standard, which, of course, includes provisions enabling it to be modified based on the specific climate zone and other regional criteria pertinent to a given project. While all homes complying with the standard will have to address all of the baseline credits, the flexibility of the tool allows a builder to emphasize certain areas by requiring a certain number of points from categories of the builder's choosing. To illustrate this point, the document says, "For example, an association in Florida will likely want to increase the point values attributed to installing an energy-efficient air conditioning system and decrease the point value associated with installing a high efficiency heating system. Similarly, in the southwestern United States, associations would probably place higher value on water efficiency measures."

As I hope has become apparent by now, interdisciplinary design is an important staple of green building and sustainable design. The holistic thinking characteristic of interdisciplinary design is emphasized within the NAHB program, although not as expansively as it is within some other rating systems. Often landscape architects or engineers are not granted large roles as the design develops in a traditional linear fashion, and are brought in after the basic concept and layout are complete.

The NAHB Standard program emphasizes holistic thinking from the onset of the project, not necessarily calling it out as interdisciplinary design, but with that intention nonetheless. This echoes the thought that "greening" a building after it has been designed is far more difficult than starting with environmental goals firmly in mind from the outset.

This holistic, systems thinking perspective also emphasizes potential synergies that can be created by looking at the project as one package. Yes, the double-paned windows may cost more, but by selecting them, the HVAC system can likely be downsized. When elements are looked at in an à la carte fashion, this notion of a symbiotic give-and-take may not even be recognized, let alone utilized to its full potential.

5.3 Structure of the National Standard

The *ICC 700-2008 National Green Building Standard* is structured similarly to the Guidelines as well as the LEED and Green Globes systems. The topics and credits are generally the same, although within the ANSI-approved Standard, there are six overarching categories. In the text that follows, each principle is discussed in detail only when there is something particularly noteworthy, or different from other criteria already covered in this book. The six categories are:

- Lot Design, Preparation, and Development (site)
- Resource Efficiency (materials)
- Energy Efficiency
- Water Efficiency
- Indoor Environmental Quality
- Operation, Maintenance, and Building Owner Education

In addition to these categories and credits, which are similar to those of other rating systems and guidelines, the NAHB also identifies applications and strategies that should be implemented in every home constructed, especially those aiming to be labeled as green. These necessities are viewed in NAHB's Standard in a similar fashion to LEED's prerequisites, although these required elements are not found in every section of the NAHB system. However, as mentioned previously, all areas must meet a baseline threshold that increases with higher levels of certification.

The National Green Building Standard has four levels of certification: bronze, silver, gold, and emerald. Despite this similarity to other rating systems, the method used to reach these various levels of certification is slightly different from the systems presented thus far. For each of the six categories (e.g., Resource Efficiency, Water Efficiency, Global Impact), a certain number of points are required within the category to achieve a rating. In other words, in addition to achieving a certain number of total points, the project must also meet certain point levels within each of the six categories. This structure of threshold points per category has no parallel (at the time of publication) in any of the other national rating systems described in this book with the exception of the recently instated minimum in LEED's Energy and Atmosphere Credit 1 (Optimize Energy Performance). (Remember that for projects registered after June 2007, at least two points need to be achieved in that credit category.) Note, however, that the minimums do occur in some of the local programs covered in the next chapter. As can be seen in the table on page 91, this minimum number of points increases as a project targets a higher certification level.

On top of the minimum number of credits required for each of the categories, an additional 50 points (bronze) or 100 points (silver, gold and emerald) must be achieved. These additional points can come in any combination from any of the six categories, without exception. This way, not only does the home have to meet minimum requirements in each section as noted in the chart, the home has to go beyond the minimum to be considered a member of the green building realm.

On the NAHB's National Green Building Program Web site there are a number of tabs at the top of the page. One tab is labeled "Green Scoring Tool," while the tab adjacent to it says "Rating Systems." This is slightly confusing. Clicking on the second tab will take you to the actual, printable, reviewable, and highlightable documents, providing text versions of both the *Model Green Homebuilding Guidelines* and the *National Green Building Standard*. The guidelines are free to download and the standard is available for order at a cost, though NAHB members do receive a discount. The Green Scoring Tool tab, on the other hand, steps you through the process of entering basic information into the rating system so that you can easily grasp how your project might fare vis-à-vis NAHB's National Standard.

5.4 Green Scoring Tool

The NAHB created the Green Scoring Tool to help ease first-timers into the green home building process. It is also integral to the green home certification process offered by the NAHB Research Center. (The Research Center is a subsidiary of NAHB that is a recognized by ANSI, IAPMO and a few other organizations as a credible third party testing and product certification provider.) Builders seeking certification must have a third party verifier inspect all green items in the home using a designers tool generated using the builders inputs into the Green Scoring Tool. Similar to the Green Globes online rating tool, the NAHB's Green Scoring Tool is an online, self-explanatory tool, designed to be user-friendly. It is free and available for use by anyone. Users of the scoring tool can choose either the National Green Building Standard or the older Guidelines for a rating system.

While required to certify a home through the NAHBGreen program, the tool is of particular value to either home builders with no local green building program to use as a reference or home builders who are constructing homes across markets and, consequently, may have issues in sticking to one set of local guidelines or another. It is free to use for both NAHB members and non-members. To take advantage of the tool, all you need to do is log on and create a user profile. Once that's done, you'll select which application you want to use – the NAHB Model Green Home Building Guidelines or the National Green Building Standard. Once you select the appropriate choice, you will create a project profile (much like the LEED and Green Globes initial project registration process) that consists of straightforward information such as project location, description, and so forth. This information can be stored for future updates and comparisons. Having entered that basic information, it's time to get into the scoring system. For our purposes, we are going to select the National Green Building Standard. At this point, the information required becomes more detailed and more technical in nature. The first screen gets you into the introduction for Lot Design and contains a considerable amount of information that needs to be digested. Do not be discouraged by the number of tabs and pull-down menus. If you take a minute to figure them out, they all make sense and the tool will begin to feel more user-friendly as you move from screen to screen.

If you find yourself confused about what information is actually being requested by a specific credit question, convenient tools are included to assist you. For example, one of the Lot Design credits states, *Choose an EPA-recognized brownfield.* What if you are just starting out and are not exactly sure what a brownfield is? A handy roll-over feature provides a "Help Tip" that contains clarifying information to help you make your decision. Additionally, the NAHB has positioned a useful box at each credit to address issues such as "How to Verify," "Intent," "How to Implement," and "Resources." These open up a smaller window in the browser to answer additional questions and provide valuable background information. These links can be a great resource for future reference or simply to broaden your knowledge about particular issues. As with all of the systems being reviewed, the scoring tool is constantly being altered and improved. While it is currently available for new single and multi-family projects and additions, it will soon address remodels and land development projects as well.

The delineation of points at each possible credit in the Scoring Tool may seem slightly simplified, but you just have to know where to look for additional clarification. For example, under Resource Efficiency > Reuse Materials, one possible credit states, *Reclaimed and/or salvaged materials and components are used. The total material and labor cost of salvaged materials is equal to or exceeds 1% of the total construction cost.* This is fairly self-explanatory and there is a note that there are three "Points Possible." The option is either to check the "Points Claimed" box or not. It looks at first like an easy judgment call, but if you dig further in the provided links addressing *How to Verify, Intent, How to Implement, Resources,* there is guidance in these categories to tell you how many of those three possible points you can claim.

The basic notion of this tool is that builders and homeowners alike can dive in to the sometimes vague land of sustainability and begin to understand what makes a green home green, as well as how to make that happen. By identifying green strategies that can be implemented in residential design and construction, the tool enables homeowners to get involved in the choices surrounding the greening of their home without having an extensive background in design, construction, or green building. The tool can provide a means of facilitating communication between homeowners and the architects and construction industry professionals who are designing and building their house at all stages of the project's development. The system also offers a relatively easy way for the general population to become educated and find ways of incorporating green strategies into their homes whether they are planning refurbishments or new construction. Once all the information has been entered into the online Green Scoring Tool, a "Project Scoring Analysis" gives a breakdown of where the project sits in relation to the four possible certification levels: bronze, silver, gold, or emerald. Four charts on the Project Scoring Analysis page show the minimum points required for certification at each level, followed by a column with the points that your project has claimed for each of the chapters. The next column lists the excess points claimed per category, which contribute toward the 100 extra points needed for certification. The last column, "Point Shortfall," shows how many points the project may be short for that level of certification. Providing a quick snapshot of where and by how much a particular project falls short in

any given category, the illustration shows the breakdown for a home at the bronze level. If the project were hovering between silver and gold, for instance, the chart would show the most fruitful places to concentrate the team's efforts in order to pick up the additional points necessary to achieve gold status.

5.5 The User Guide

To support successful use of the rating systems under NAHBGreen, NAHB created a User Guide contained in the Guidelines and is developing companion commentary for the National Green Building Standard, which will expand on the intents of the measures within it, guidance on complying with these measures and suggested external resources for additional information. The Commentary for the Standard is expected to be published in 2009. Practically speaking, the User Guide within the Model Green Homebuilding Guidelines resembles the LEED Reference Guide in intent and format. A handy document, the User Guide attempts to answer the questions likely to arise when using the ratings system. As was noted in the discussion of the Green Globes system, these questions are not always adequately addressed. With the Green Globes system, some credits are explained with only a sentence or two when more clarification is probably warranted. In contrast, for each credit noted in *Model Green Homebuilding Guidelines*, the NAHB elaborates on the intent of the credit, provides additional information about how to achieve the credit, and lists additional resources that may be useful in integrating and pursuing the credit. Helpful to any project, this information is particularly beneficial to a team that is just beginning to learn about how to build green buildings.

5.6 Certification and Verification Process

As mentioned earlier, the NAHB Guidelines have been adapted and modified by many local HBAs to speak specifically to their climate and region. In these cases, the local HBA is meant to be the keeper and moderator of these adapted guidelines and a resource in helping those in their region to follow the guidelines successfully. But what do you do if there is no local HBA in your area? Or it hasn't yet jumped onto the green bandwagon and so there doesn't seem to be anyone around moderating this initiative? To address this issue, the NAHB launched the National program in 2008. A key goal of the national program is to provide third-party verification in areas where none previously existed. The new approach allows every builder access to a credible-yet-flexible, nationally recognized third party green certification.

The certification process is relatively simple. As previously stated, it starts during the design process with the online scoring tool, and the completion of the online checklist. Each credit on the online Green Scoring Tool has a link to a sidebar, "How to Verify" And each of the verification links tells you exactly what needs to be done *when* and confirmed *how* for your project to become officially certified at some level. Once a certifiable score (bronze through emerald) has been achieved,

the user then gets a Designers Report and contacts one of the NAHB Research Center Accredited Verifiers found on www.nahbgreen.org. Accredited verifiers are independent service providers trained by the NAHB Research Center. As of this writing several hundred individual verifiers were listed across all states, each servicing a regional zone, so there should be no difficulty finding one regardless of where in the United States your project may be located. These verifiers are independent contractors and their service fees are independently negotiated with each builder. The verifier's role is to perform inspections using the Designers Report as a home's customized green checklist. Verifiers perform at least two onsite inspections and acquire any needed documentation from the builder. Once all points have been confirmed in the field, the Verifier communicates with the NAHB Research Center in Maryland for review.

The NAHB Research Center is the only group that can certify a home under the NAHBGreen program. After the Research Center validates the information from the third-party verifier and collects the certification fee, the center issues a certificate for the home and builders have the option of showcasing the home on NAHBGree.org. Keep in mind that this verification element is required for the NAHBGreen program and any local programs affiliated with NAHBGreen, but not necessarily for any of the non-affiliated HBA guidelines that may have been created and administered locally. If the local HBA decides that verification is necessary, it will provide third-party verification guidelines that have been established within their local organization and comply with their specific requirements.

At the national level, NAHB's objective is to make the process as user-friendly and cost-effective as possible with the idea that available dollars saved on administrative costs will either go toward more green features or a lower priced home. Verification for non-NAHBGreen programs may be handled differently with respect to fees; these, if there are any, would be set by the local program and may vary significantly from one program to another.

6: Local Green Building Guidelines

In addition to the nationally organized green building guidelines reviewed in the previous chapters (and others not covered in this book), a number of localities have taken it upon themselves to create and implement their own version of green building guidelines. This chapter provides an overview of seven different local green building strategies or programs from regions across the United States. If you are not in one of these regions, I encourage you to find out what your specific locality is doing—or help get a program started if none exists.

J. Matt Thomas, a colleague, completed a study in 2005 for the City of Santa Fe's Department of Affordable Housing, which was interested in starting its own set of local green building guidelines. Thomas's study concentrated primarily on localities in the West, inching over to the middle of the country. Several examples in this chapter stem from his work. The other examples, from the East Coast and Midwest, were gathered specifically for this book, using Thomas's format and criteria as a model. Because local guidelines can vary considerably from one another, I have taken a broad-brush rather than an in-depth approach to describing and comparing them.

The localities whose guidelines are summarized in this chapter are listed below. Austin comes first because it was the first local program developed in the U.S. The remaining places are presented in alphabetical order. The Web addresses provided connect you either with specific green building programs for that locality or, in the absence of a locally specific site, with an alternate source of useful information to support your interest in green building:

- Austin, TX www.austinenergy.com
- Arlington, VA www.arlingtonva.us
- North Carolina www.healthybuilthomes.org
- Portland, OR www.portandonline.com/bps
- Santa Monica, CA www.smgreen.org

- Scottsdale, AZ www.scottsdaleaz.gov
/greenbuilding
- Wisconsin www.wi-ei.org

These are by no means the only places making great strides with local green building guidelines and initiatives. As you read the program descriptions and the comparative discussion that follows them and concludes this book, keep in mind that these are only a sampling of the growing possibilities in the field of green building.

6.1 Austin, Texas

Starting a bit earlier than many other places—and with fierce dedication and a specific set of goals in mind—Austin, Texas, quickly became a measuring stick for other programs to use and modify as appropriate to local considerations.

**AUSTIN ENERGY
GREEN BUILDING**

6.1.1 Organization Overview

Austin's green building initiatives were trendsetters from the outset. No conversation about local green building programs of note would be complete without including the Texas capital. Austin's affinity for green building may be fed by a number of factors: its role as the state capital and site of the high-tech University of Texas; its diverse and cultured population, includ-

ing a large creative class; and its progressive, largely forward-thinking community.

As early as 1991, Austin took green building and sustainability to heart when it developed an independent Green Building Program. The initiative started with an ENERGY STAR program, created by the city council in 1985 and focused on energy conservation in response to the intended construction of a new power plant in the area. Not just a basic nod to green building and energy conservation methods, the Green Building Program won an award for Local Government Initiatives at the 1992 United Nations Earth Summit in Rio de Janeiro, barely a year after its introduction.

In 1991, the Green Building Program developed a residential rating tool (described in Section 6.1.3 below) and then, in 1992, published its first Sustainable Building Sourcebook, encouraging the Austin city council to pass a resolution to include green building measures in city facilities and projects. A charter member of the U.S. Green Building Council, the Green Building Program also developed guidelines for municipal projects, establishing a Commercial Green Building Program in 1995 (described in section 6.1.4 below).

Three years later, in 1998, the Green Building Program was pulled under the umbrella of Austin Energy, which now owns and oversees the program. Established in 1895, Austin Energy is a community-owned electric utility housed within the city of Austin. The utility's savings and profits are given back to the community as funds for public services including police, libraries, fire protection, and parks. While the Green Building Program had been making strides on its own, partnering with Austin Energy gave the movement even more vitality and muscle to advance its initiatives.

6.1.2 Offerings

Since those early and fruitful beginnings, Austin Energy Green Building™ (AEGB) has developed a number of additional programs, documents, and initiatives. These tools, although developed to be specific to the Austin area, can also be used and/or adapted as a template for others hoping to launch green building programs around the country. An overview of several of AEGB's many offerings precedes the description of its primary guidelines so you can look for parallels in your own region and, where none exist, encourage their development. Here are just a few of the resources available from Austin Energy Green Building:

- *The Sustainable Building Sourcebook*: 50+ Topics
  This reference guide focuses on the regional and local specifics of Austin, emphasizing strategies and elements that might be used there. It is not a technical construction manual, but a handbook to help guide projects and professionals in appropriate directions as designs progress. The Sourcebook is meant to be an overview that helps get a team started on the right foot by understanding how the intricacies of Austin's climate and region, and other factors, affect green building design. Anyone who works in Austin or is planning to build there should refer to this document as a resource; interactive options and updates are in development. The information may also be applicable for development in other hot, humid climates.

- Green by Design Workshops
  Geared toward homeowners, these workshops are held four times a year and focus on the seven steps to green building. The program enables local residents to increase the water efficiency, energy efficiency, comfort, and durability of their homes. There is a small fee to attend the workshop. In addition to a full day of instruction from the pros at Austin Energy, workshop participants receive a workbook for future reference, engage in a Q&A session with local building professionals, and receive product samples from local eco-friendly businesses. Topics covered include determining what a family needs in its home, how to select a builder or designer, how to reduce utility bills while increasing comfort, what to consider when selecting building materials and appliances, low-maintenance landscaping, and

understanding the particular lot in order to best site the house.

- Consulting and educational services for those in the building industry
- Professional directory
- Events calendar
- Marketing seminar series, including AIA Learning Units
- Austin's Green Map (highlighting local green projects)
- Local rebates and loans for conservation tactics through Austin Energy
- Manage it Green—a consulting service based on helping other municipalities, utilities, and government agencies develop local green building programs that address their local needs
- Case studies
- Rating systems—several versions are available, depending on the type of project: residential, commercial, and multi-family

6.1.3 Austin Energy Green Building Residential Program

AEGB's Residential Program outreach efforts target mainly home builders. The Residential Program rating system is designed to rate both new and remodeled homes on a scale of one to five stars, the more stars the better.

The Single-Family Home rating covers six main categories:

- Energy efficiency
- Testing
- Water efficiency
- Materials efficiency
- Health and safety
- Community

In order to actually use the residential guidelines, the designer, builder, or architect must attend an orientation and work with AEGB throughout design and construction. At the time of writing, there was no fee associated with receiving a rating if the project is in the Austin Energy service area.

6.1.4 Austin Energy Green Building Commercial Program

Unlike the Residential Program, the Commercial Program guides projects through a performance-based path to achieve a rating. This approach emphasizes green building goal-setting early in the design process and monitoring throughout the life of the project. The rating packet includes helpful sections including Project Information, Project Team, Worksheet, and Rating Report, which include more detailed calculation elements such as Building Reuse, Construction Waste, Water, Irrigation, Building Materials, Low VOC, and Certified Wood. Each of the larger sections (listed first) describes the data that need to be gathered for specific strategies; the more detailed calculations are used to track progress. The larger sections help to outline a processes that the team may want to use to achieve their green building goals, as well as how to best communicate strategies, milestones, and next steps among team members.

AEGB's Commercial Program encourages teams to involve AEGB staff as an integrated member of the design team, helping to guide the project and other team members along the path to achieving the project's green building goals. An AEGB professional serves as a green building consultant and might, on any project, suggest appropriate materials, orientation, and systems, as well as encourage each project team to meet and exceed its goals for other considerations. Among those are energy and water, pollution control, conservation tactics, and even occupant productivity. As with other AEGB programs, the organization's Commercial Program staff helps to market the projects on which they consult throughout the community.

6.1.5 Austin Energy Green Building Multi-Family Program

One of a handful of specifically multi-family programs in the United States, AEGB's Multi-Family Program focuses on apartments and condos that are less than seven stories above ground. The rating packet is designed similarly to the one used by the Commercial Program and allows for flexibility as project teams select either prescriptive or performance-based paths throughout the rating. Like the Commercial Program, the Multi-Family Program also engages AEGB staff as sustainability consultants on each project pursuing a rating. The services provided range from goal-setting early in the design process to construction document review and onsite consultation. When a project achieves a rating from the Multi-Family Program, it also receives assistance in marketing the project to the public.

6.1.6 Additional Austin Energy Initiatives and Incentives

In addition to the benefits and initiatives described above, Austin Energy helps projects gain access to incentives for electric, gas, and water conservation. For energy efficiency alone, Austin Energy provides links to a number of incentive, rebate, and guidance programs. These include a Power Saver™ Program that focuses on energy within the home. A free online home energy analysis, available through the program, provides advice to homeowners on how a given home uses energy, how it compares with other homes in the area, and ways to save on utility bills. Homeowners have an opportunity to be Power Partners—members of a program that provides residents with a Power Partner programmable thermostat in exchange for allowing the air conditioner to be "cycled off" for ten minutes during peak times, thus reducing the load on energy generation.

Another residential offering that helps support energy efficiency is the Duct Diagnostic Program, which addresses both the amount of air leakage that occurs in an older home and the reduced level of air quality that leaky homes can create. The onsite analysis identifies any notable leaks in the ductwork, unsafe carbon monoxide levels, and air-flow levels to individual rooms, as well as what the return air vents are bringing into the home.

For commercial clients, there are tips on energy-saving data centers for companies or corporations, and possible energy rebates for these facilities up to $200,000. There is also a directory of participating companies whose services range from solar screens to window film, roof coating, chillers, solar power, and solar thermal water heaters. A comparable directory of residentially appropriate resources is also provided for the housing sector.

Additional energy efficiency resources in the Austin area include renewable energy offerings with an emphasis on solar power. Like many other locales, Austin offers subscriptions to a green power source, allowing homeowners and companies alike to support clean and renewable power sources. Most of Austin Energy's 665 million kilowatt hours (kWh) of green power comes from wind turbines in west Texas, but a portion also comes from several solar and three landfill gas projects. The GreenChoice charge replaces the regular fuel charge; at the time of writing, Austin Energy was offering its fifth batch at 5.5 cents per kWh guaranteed until the end of 2022.

Further, the Power Saver Program offers rebates on a number of possible residential and commercial energy-saving options. On the residential side as of year-end 2008, there are rebates relating to ENERGY STAR Home Performance, air conditioning, programmable thermostats, solar photovoltaics, and solar water heaters. Commercially (also, as of year-end 2008), there are offerings for commercial energy management, data center efficiency, small businesses, energy misers (vending machines), programmable thermostats, solar photovoltaics, solar water heaters, thermal energy storage, energy demand management during peak times (Load Co-op), building commissioning (measurement and verification of the systems), and specific incentives for implementing energy improvements for multi-family complexes.

As if those initiatives were not enough, Austin Energy also helps homeowners through ENERGY STAR low-interest loans. These loans can cover a variety of energy-efficient home improvements including:

- installing a new energy-efficient air conditioner or heat pump
- supplementing the existing attic insulation
- repairing leaky ductwork
- caulking around and under sink fixtures
- weather stripping around doors
- installing low-E glazing, awnings, or solar screens
- installing attic radiant barrier reflective material

With these initiatives and more, it is understandable how Austin has come to be a leader in local green building initiatives and has the top-performing renewable energy program in the nation. It is not only the first but also the largest local green building program in the country.

6.2 Arlington, Virginia

Because of the availability of a number of proven and highly regarded national green building programs (such as the ones described in this book), many local jurisdictions are deciding to use such programs as the favored standards for projects in their area. Arlington, Virginia, is one such place.

Arlington County has pledged that all of its public buildings will achieve a LEED Silver rating. Additional support for green building is seen in the county's "site plan project" program, which allows developers to apply for zoning exceptions to increase flexibility in their projects. Any project applying for an exception to the Zoning Ordinance (which covers any large office, residential, or mixed-use project) must specifically include all of the following: a LEED Accredited Professional, a LEED Scorecard, a Construction Waste Management Plan, ENERGY STAR fixtures (for multi-family housing), and participation in Arlington County's Green Building Fund. The donation at the time of writing, set at $0.045 per square foot, is refunded if the project receives LEED certification. If the proj-

ARLINGTON
VIRGINIA

ect does not achieve LEED certification, the donation is kept by the county and used for green building education and outreach within the Arlington community.

6.2.1 Commercial Incentives

Another way to make a project stand out within its locality and to encourage green building is to offer incentives if it adheres to some version of green building guidelines. Arlington, for example, implemented its first pilot Green Building Incentive Program in 2000, based on the then-current version of LEED. In 2003, after several years of feedback and refinement, Arlington developed the Green Building Density Incentive Program. This program had input from a number of different city departments, including but not limited to Environmental Services; Community Planning, Housing, and Development; Economic Development; the Arlington County Manager's Office; and the Arlington County Attorney's Office. The program is scheduled for review every five years or as needed based on market demand. It was updated in early 2009 based on data from 2003–8.

To be eligible for the incentive program, a project must be seeking some level of LEED certification. In exchange for the dedication to LEED certification, projects may be granted extra density or height, though neither is guaranteed. Each project is reviewed on a case-by-case basis before it can be granted additional density.

6.2.2 Residential

Another set of guidelines developed in Arlington County is the Green Home Choice Program* (http://www.arlingtonva.us/departments/EnvironmentalServices/epo/EnvironmentalServicesEpoGreenHomeChoice.aspx). These guidelines address the county's residential market, a sector in which other green building guidelines have yet to gain a stronghold. The program is geared to home builders (as opposed to owners) to encourage companies to join the green building movement. Some of the incentives offered to motivate home builders to participate in the Green Home Choice Program include expedited plan reviews, green building seminars, recognition as a green builder, and a lawn sign that proclaims the home's status as a sustainable building.

At the outset of the process, when the home builder decides to pursue a green home, the builder must contact the Arlington County Environmental Planning Office to state formally that intention and sign an Intent Form. The plans are then identified as a "green home" project. A green home inspector is assigned to the project to ensure that the green home components are appropriately included in the construction.

The Green Home Choice Program was modeled after the Earthcraft House Program (www.earthcrafthouse.com) created by Southface Institute in Atlanta, Georgia (www.southface.org). Established as a voluntary program for home builders, the program is outlined in a guidance document, available online, which outlines the various green components that can be included in a green residence project. The topics are categorized into common construction concepts such as Site Planning, Energy Efficient Building Envelope and Systems, Energy Efficient Appliances and Lighting, Resource Efficient Building Materials, and Waste Management. While these are not all of the primary categories, the sampling is enough to illustrate the concerns that this program has in common with the other green building guidelines described in this book.

The main categories are broken down further into more specific sections, each with its own set of criteria. For example, the Resource Efficient Building Materials category includes such subcategories as Recycled and Natural Content Materials, Advanced Products (such as engineered flooring or prefabricated panels), and Durability.

The subcategories are broken down even further into specific points to work toward within the guidelines. For example, under the Recycled and Natural Content Materials subcategory, the Recycled Content Tiles guideline requires that a minimum of 50 percent of tile floors shall contain at least 30 percent recycled material content; documentation is required. The criteria are simple and spelled out in an extremely straightforward manner—no additional guidelines, references, or precedents; no resources to

---

*At the time of writing, the version of the Arlington Green Home Choice Program document on the Web site was dated June 18, 2003.

use or further points to research. The only thing left to do (other than actually complying with the targeted initiatives, of course) is to record that compliance on the Arlington Green Home Choice Scoring Worksheet and submit it for certification review.

6.2.3 Scoring Worksheet

The program offers only one level of certification: the Arlington Green Home Choice Certification Award, for which a project must earn 175 points. A scoring worksheet is used to calculate the point totals. Using the guidance document and worksheet, a home builder can categorize and outline the steps that were taken when designing and building the home being submitted for green certification. The worksheet and guidance document can be downloaded from the Green Home Choice Web site.

The first page of the worksheet deals with project logistics and contact information: builder, contact person, contact information, address of the home, square footage of the home, and so on. There is also a statement, to be signed by the builder, confirming that the home will adhere to the specifications and requirements set forth in the subsequent pages of the worksheet.

In addition to the basic information, the first page addresses the development and approval of a homeowner manual to be distributed to home buyers upon purchase. This procedure, common in many local residential programs, highlights the importance of education within green building. Creating a high-performance building that can save energy and exist lightly on the land is the essential first step. But if users are not aware of how to operate the systems to maximize the benefits, the potential for energy savings, durability, and maintenance of materials could be totally wasted, or at the least severely diminished. If inappropriate cleaners are used on specific surfaces, they may deteriorate more rapidly and need to be replaced more frequently, negating the intended results. To support home buyers in achieving these green goals, the creation and dissemination of a homeowner's manual is a prerequisite for certification.

The rest of the worksheet is divided into four columns: the credit (e.g., permeable paving materials), the points allotted to that strategy, the score achieved, and the means of documentation. Many of the point allotments are straightforward, i.e., a fixed number of points (1, 2, 3); others may be designated as 1–4 or 1+. Scoring is explained in the description of the intended strategy in the guidance document. For example, the points attainable for Site Planning > Tree Preservation and Enhancement > Tree Canopy Enhancement are listed as 1–4. The guidance document describes that strategy: *Add one point for each 5% increment above the minimum canopy requirement of 20% 20-year post development. Newly planted trees may be used to determine this calculation (up to 4 extra points available).* This notation clearly explains the opportunity to earn additional points and how to achieve them.

Each of the primary sections on the worksheet has a place

to total the credits for that section, and on the last page of the worksheet is a section in which to tally those subtotals and create a grand total for the home. Once the worksheet has been completed, the builder compiles the necessary documentation for each applied strategy and submits the entire package for review and a final inspection by an Arlington County Green Home Choice inspector. After review and approval, certification is awarded.

6.2.4 Additional Resources

Additional resources on Arlington County's Green Home Choice Web site include a list of builders and other professionals who have participated in the program: Contractors and Builders, Architects, Landscape Designers, Building Service Specialists, and Green Products Suppliers. A list of Green Building Resources for the public includes the EPA's ENERGY STAR Program, *Natural Home* magazine, *Environmental Design and Construction* magazine, and many others.

Links to Related Resources include a three-part slideshow from a presentation on Green Remodeling as well as a link to the Green Guide (a blog hosted by National Geographic). In addition, the Related Resources link the Arlington County Green Building Program to larger issues of sustainability, addressing such issues as green living, buying guides, even green weddings!

The Arlington County approach to local green building guidelines is a solid program that takes advantage of some of the more established national programs, such as LEED and ENERGY STAR, and fills any remaining perceived gaps with other solid examples (such as Atlanta's Earthcraft House Program) that fit the county's needs. This allows not only for standardization and comparisons with other municipalities in the commercial sector, but also for ingenuity and fine-tuning incentives locally. Other localities around the country also adapt and adopt to suit their particular needs, as can be seen in the program descriptions that follow.

6.3 North Carolina

In 2008, North Carolina ranked sixth nationally in quantity of new housing, making the state a market ripe for sustainability and green building initiatives. Until the economic downturn in the second half of 2008, residential development throughout the 100 counties in North Carolina was booming and, it is hoped, will again once the economy recovers. The boom may be partially due to the major universities and research parks located in North Carolina, or the fact that many residents are within driving distance of the natural beauty found in the state's many beaches, state parks, and mountains. Whatever the reason, growth in the residential market of North Carolina means opportunities for green building throughout the state.

The burgeoning population of North Carolina has put the

primary green building focus and rating system development in the state squarely on the residential market. HealthyBuilt Homes (discussed below in section 6.3.1) originated before many other green guidelines and, as a result, thoroughly establishes a baseline for residential building within the state and region. A network of small business has flourished around, and in support of, this system. Among the many businesses that have emerged are those providing residential energy audits, rain barrel design and installation, and indoor mold and air quality management. This is a great example of how green can help boost the local economy.

6.3.1 The North Carolina HealthyBuilt Homes Program

The North Carolina HealthyBuilt Homes Program (HBH), unlike others around the country, historically does not market itself as "green" because the program was created before the term was popular and understood by the residential market. Instead, the program emphasizes the well-being fostered by the resultant residence for both the occupants and the environment. The initiative was developed and is administered and maintained by the North Carolina Solar Center at North Carolina State University in partnership with the State Energy Office. Local building professional organizations such as home builders associations across the state provide feedback and information to the program. In Asheville, for example, the local home builders association works as a Community Partner.

The primary goal of the HBH Program is to support and educate small- to medium-sized homebuilders and others in the building industry as they take their first steps into the green building market. HBH also serves larger builders interested in participating in the program.

HealthyBuilt Homes works to create a viable residential green building industry in North Carolina by first providing affordable educational services to builders. These services include such things as design reviews, workshops, marketing and technical assistance, and even field consultations. HBH's ultimate goal is to focus less on some of the specific services once a strong market has been created and to transition the organization to focus more on quality assurance of the new "green industry." An example of this intended organizational move toward a quality assurance role can be found in its creation of the HBH Independent Inspector Member category; these private consultants are currently in training at the North Carolina Solar Center. They will be tapping into a new market, helping builders by providing the green building field consultations that HBH personnel currently complete.

The HealthyBuilt Homes program was developed in 2002–3 through a statewide task force of interested building professionals. Task force members began reaching out directly to other builders in 2004. For example, the HBH director in place as of this writing is an architect who in private practice places great emphasis on low-impact architecture. In 2000, through a contact at Austin Energy's Green Building Program, she began looking for an opportunity to plug into a green building program. In 2001, synergy occurred when the Solar Center wanted to create a solar hot water program with the financial support of the State Energy Office. Maintained and supported by North Carolina State University's Solar Center Building Team, HBH continues to grow in scope and application.

Stressing that homes are systems, not just a collection of parts, the HBH program pays attention to most aspects of residential construction. The program name, first checklist, and reference manual were developed and refined using feedback from both home building and high performance building professionals. The program found its initial niche in western North Carolina, the location of HBH's first multi-home project.

In 2008, western North Carolina accounted for more than half of the program's enrollment and home registrations. HealthyBuilt Homes has also seen rapid growth in Mecklenburg County (Charlotte) and the Wilmington area. As of June 2008, HBH had grown to 117 builder members, 7 Independent Inspector members in training, 229 registered homes, and 159 certified homes at various levels.

Because the HBH program is a statewide program dependent on regional support and even, at times, local expertise, HBH has created a Community Partner program that is an integral part of HBH's outreach and support to various groups. The HBH Community Partner, specific to different cities in the state, enrolls local organizations dedicated to sustainability and high-performance building to support the HBH Statewide Partner. The Statewide Partner in turn serves as the primary regional contact and staff person for HBH. Statewide HBH staff (the Building Team at the Solar Center) provide quality control, program integrity, and development functions and also cover areas of the state that do not have a Community Partner, so all North Carolinians have access to green home certification and support. In mid-2007, it became apparent that there were not enough local groups available and willing to take on this effort, especially as national programs began to enter the residential green construction market. As of mid-2008, there were two HBH Community Partners: Western North Carolina Green Building Council in Asheville, which administers NC Healthy-Built Homes of Greater Asheville, and Appalachian State University's Energy Center, which administers NC HealthyBuilt Homes of Northwestern North Carolina.

6.3.2 Markets Served

The primary audience for the North Caorlina HealthyBuilt Homes Program consists of members of the residential construction industry; the goal is to shift the industry toward sustainability. That notwithstanding, HBH is also designed to appeal to a number of other groups, including home buyers, designers, energy raters, suppliers, lenders, property appraisers, and realtors. The HealthyBuilt Homes Web site (www.

healthybuilthomes.org) targets each of these groups by providing tailored information about why they would want to be involved and how they can best get involved. Simple and concise, the Web site provides extensive resources to its users.

The benefits to builders and developers are fairly similar once they enroll as members for a small annual fee. As with other programs, membership allows builders to access some of the incentives mentioned above, such as an introductory training on the HBH system, free topic workshops, market development materials such as brochures and logos, consultations, and a "feature" spot on the HBH Web site.

The program for home owners and home buyers includes an online list of HBH builders by county. The list provides the name, address, and Web site for each home builder, the number of HBH homes each has in progress, and the number of certified HBH projects, grouped by certification level. A Web gallery of homes consists of case studies showing images of select HBH homes and their key features. This visual aspect can be very helpful to interested individuals who are not necessarily well versed in the home building industry. An additional benefit is a link to the North Carolina Professional Directory, also hosted by the North Carolina Solar Center. The directory focuses on sustainable building professionals in the state (www.greenprofessionals.org) with links on the "News" page to green building stories and other applicable articles in newspapers and other media. Links to HBH events can be found on the "Calendar" page; and connections to a variety of sources such as national financial resources, products and materials, general green building resources, home maintenance resources, and real estate resources, among others, are on the "Links" page. Anyone interested in looking for a greener home will find the "Links" page an excellent place to begin their research.

The site also has information of use to building-related professionals such as suppliers, lenders, and realtors. Each area of the site—Supplier, Lender, Realtor—has its own slant and a description of the ways in which those building professionals can become involved with the HBH program. For example, suppliers are provided with information on how to sponsor the HBH program and connect with HBH builders who may be interested in the suppliers' products. Qualified suppliers are also presented with the opportunity to be listed in the professional directory. The Lender area directs visitors to various loan programs, utility incentives, and available financing products that visitors may find valuable when assessing the financing of an HBH certified green home. The Realtor section focuses primarily on marketing tools as well as directing visitors to this page toward energy raters and HBH builders.

6.3.3 Additional Resources

A number of additional resources are available through the HBH program. One example is a Product Selection Guide compiled by the North Carolina Solar Center. It is a single-page fact sheet in PDF form and outlines "3 Basic Steps for High Performance Product Selection" that are helpful to designers, contractors, builders, owners, and suppliers. The Product Selection Guide aligns closely with an overview of various product certification guides that speak more to the supplier and manufacturer's perspectives. A number of the most well-known product certifiers are accessible through links on the Suppliers page.

Another resource found on the HBH Web site is a link to the North Carolina Green Building Technology Database. Also hosted by the Solar Center, the database provides case studies of green building techniques, strategies, and technologies. Projects presented in the case studies are all located in North Carolina. The technologies used for these projects are searchable by technique, location, building type, or site condition. The information is helpful as a source of ideas for successful implementation of green strategies and as possible field trips for firsthand observation.

6.3.4 North Carolina HealthyBuilt Homes Program Statewide Checklist

HBH's Checklist and its Reference Manual—the meat of the HBH program—are available online for anyone to peruse at no charge. Version 3.0, current as of this writing, was released in July 2006. The general structure is the same as other rating systems that have been reviewed; there are prerequisites and categories of "Opportunities" with minimum point requirements in each category. The ratings scale is as follows:

> 100–150 points: Certified (a minimum of 100 points is required for certification)
> 151–200 points: Bronze certified
> 201–250 points: Silver certified
> 251+ points: Gold certified

The checklist is a sixteen-page spreadsheet, broken out in typical fashion with space in front of each credit to indicate the

---

Product Certifications: *While, as noted in Chapter 2, USGBC does not certify products (and you should be wary of sales reps or organizations that claim that their product is LEED certified), there are organizations that do certify different categories of products. The Forrest Stewardship Council is one (lumber products). Others include Green Guard (low-emitting interior materials and building construction guides for preventing mold), Green Seal (cleaners, floor care, paints, paper, windows, etc.), and the Cool Roof Rating Council (radiative property data on roof surfaces). The Carpet and Rug Institute (CRI) rates flooring and cleaning products. These are just a few of the organizations that certify specific products, helping green builders achieve their goals.*

intention to use that credit and the status of completion. A seventy-five-page Reference Manual supports successful use of the checklist by presenting in-depth information for each credit. Each "Opportunity" is detailed out with "Expected Documentation," which explains what is required to achieve the credit; and "Information," which may be a few short paragraphs on steps probably needed to achieve the credit. The "Information" section may include some explanation of terms or methods, but the instructions are by and large prescriptive in tone, explaining how to do what needs to be done.

An "Intent" column in the Reference Manual contains a simple statement about the objective of the credit, as well as a column for additional "Resources." Both are fairly simple in content. The "Resources" column provides Web links and additional documents for reference; the "Intent" box typically contains a statement stating, "This checklist item is intended to give a project credit for promoting . . ." or "Intended to give credit for . . ." The statements may end with ". . . providing effective spot ventilation" or ". . . recycling." The additional reasoning and supporting information about why effective spot ventilation is important is provided on request by HBH staff and included in the topic workshops that are an integral part of the educational portion of the program. When a builder joins the HBH program, the builder has access to a "live" linked version of the Reference Manual for easy access, showing that the HBH program is geared primarily toward those in the building profession and specifically those already interested in, and at least slightly familiar with, environmentally friendly concepts.

The HBH rating system compiles all the required measures (prerequisites) at the beginning of the manual. Most of these requirements deal with energy efficiency via ENERGY STAR, HVAC, air barriers, and indoor air quality. The Opportunities sections established for the HBH program contain what you'd expect, although with an obvious emphasis on energy usage going beyond ENERGY STAR, which has already been deemed "baseline" by Prerequisite 2. The eight established Opportunity categories and their subcategories are:

- Site: Soil Amendments; Vegetation; and Development (minimum 7 points)
- Water: Outdoor; Indoor (minimum 9 points)
- Energy, Building Envelope: Air Filtration; Insulation: Window and Doors (minimum 10 points)
- Energy, Comfort Systems: Passive Solar Heating and Cooling Strategies; Mechanical Comfort Systems (ductwork); Mechanical Comfort Systems (equipment) (minimum 18 points)
- Energy: Appliances; Lighting; Renewables (minimum 10 points)
- Indoor Air Quality: Structural Air Quality; Appliance Air Quality; IAQ Material Use (minimum 15 points)

- Material Opportunities: Construction Material Waste; Exterior/Structural System Materials; Interior Materials (minimum 18 points)
- Bonus (minimum 2 points)

The above list indicates that there is a little more emphasis on energy within this rating system than in some of the others reviewed. From the combination of the three categories dealing with energy, a minimum of 38 points is required.

To understand the underlying intent of the HBH system, it is worth noting that the original concept for both the Site and Water sections included a Community section for each Community Partner that focused on regionally specific items, such as land development and local water use. The Greater Asheville Community Partner Program has implemented Community items in the Site and Water sections of the checklist, while the Northwestern North Carolina program has not. Currently, the choice of how to implement items of this type is left up to the locality.

As the HBH program moves forward, however, the Site and Water sections are being rewritten to play a stronger role in the larger statewide checklist because of the addition of Independent Inspectors who may or may not work within a Community Partner in the HBH program. This will take the Site and Water sections back from the localities and make them more uniform throughout the state. HBH Independent Inspectors are being used by the Solar Center to create a stronger impact while keeping a small staff in Raleigh at the Solar Center. The Independent Inspectors are Home Energy Raters who have been sought out for their level of training, testing experience, and the quality control of their work within the framework of the HBH program. These inspectors are further qualified through classroom and field training from the Solar Center, covering all HBH program criteria including the local intricacies of the Site and Water sections.

6.4 Portland, Oregon

Portland is well known as a progressive and environmentally friendly city, so it should come as no surprise that it is a front-runner in locally implemented green building programs.

The city of Portland has adopted national guidelines for any project that receives funding or assistance from the city,

City of Portland Bureau of
Planning and Sustainability
Sam Adams, Mayor | Susan Anderson, Director

specifically from the urban development department known as the Portland Development Commission (PDC). Note, however, that there are two strands of policy: that of the city and that of the PDC. The City Council authorized the first Green Building Policy in 2001, updated it in 2005, and was updating it again at the time of writing. The same timeline applies to PDC. The scope of the city policy is city government buildings; PDC's Green Building Policy applies to private developments that receive a minimum level of city/PDC funding. The PDC policy also applies to for-profit and non-profit affordable housing projects that get PDC financing. As of April 2009, PDC's policy has resulted in twenty buildings being LEED certified; these constitute one-third of the LEED certified buildings in Portland. The criteria are reviewed below in section 6.4.1.

The other municipal department of great importance in Portland's green building movement has been the Office of Sustainable Development (OSD), which at the beginning of 2009 merged with the Bureau of Planning to become the Bureau of Planning and Sustainability (BPS). This department has historically housed the Green Building Program, which encourages the movement by offering technical assistance, courses, guidebooks, tours, and incentives to those interested in green building. There are also a number of other offerings through the new Bureau of Planning and Sustainability, which go beyond building methods. These are reviewed below in section 6.4.2.

6.4.1 PDC Green Building Policy Program Guidelines

Up to this point, I have provided an overview of how different state governments are encouraging green building through policy creation. Portland, in contrast, has developed a more focused and pared-down version of green building policy that emphasizes the city and regional levels.

The PDC policy was adopted by the PDC's Board of Commissioners in late June 2005. Portland's Green Building Policy

> **Earth Advantage:** Earth Advantage (www.earthadvantage.com) is a nonprofit organization based in the northwest United States with a branch office in Boston. The organization has shifted from an energy conservation focus based within a utility to a more holistic green building program. Like other certification processes, Earth Advantage involves a review of plans and specified materials and construction methods, construction consultations, a walk-through, performance testing upon completion of the project, and final approval and certification. The organization also offers access to green mortgages, remodeling guidelines, educational courses, and events.

Program Guidelines are mandatory for private buildings and developments receiving financial support from the PDC (the

city's department of economic development). Specifically, a project needs to be at least 10,000 square feet and receive at least 10 percent (equivalent to $300,000) in funding from the PDC to make these guidelines a requirement.

In the realm of new construction, city-owned buildings

are required by a separate city policy to achieve LEED for New Construction Gold certification, as well as implementing either "ecoroof" or ENERGY STAR–approved roofing. Commercial, mixed-use, and residential projects (equal to or over five stories) are required to achieve LEED for New Construction Silver certification. Other residential projects of less than five stories must achieve Earth Advantage Green certification (see the sidebar). Any commercial or mixed-use new construction projects that receive support from the PDC are also required to achieve LEED Silver certification.

In Portland, five-story residential projects require either Earth Advantage certification or LEED for New Construction Silver certification, depending on the specific shape and layout of the building. All multi-family affordable residential projects, regardless of size, must adhere to Portland's Green Affordable Housing Guide, considered below in section 6.4.4.

For rehabilitation and renovation projects, similar criteria must be met. For example, in a commercial or mixed-use project, LEED for New Construction Silver certification would be mandatory for the rehabilitation of an entire building. If the project entailed only an upfit (tenant improvements) or the partial renovation of a building, LEED for Commercial Interiors (CI) Silver certification and/or the local Green Building Program Tenant Improvement Guide certification (discussed below in section 6.4.4) would be required. For city-owned buildings, either LEED-CI Silver certification or Green Building Program Tenant Improvement Guide certification is required. Portland's approach shows how localities can capitalize on national standards while still allowing for local incentives and guidelines to contribute to forwarding green building in their area.

6.4.2 Portland's Bureau of Planning and Sustainability

The city of Portland founded the Office of Sustainable Development (OSD) in September 2000 by uniting its Department of Solid Waste and Recycling with the Energy Office. The mission of the OSD has been "to provide leadership and contribute practical solutions to ensure a prosperous community where people and nature thrive, now and in the future." While the scope of this mission incorporates a more holistic perspective of sustainability than strictly green building, the programs and policies offered still focus primarily on quantitative endeavors including:

- Energy Conservation, Renewable Energy, and Biofuels—These efforts encourage municipal programs to secure 100 percent of their energy from renewable sources, increase tax credits and incentives, and create and implement a biofuels strategy in the region.
- Solid Waste and Recycling—The emphasis is on reducing waste within the city and adjacent counties.
- Global Warming—The goal is to motivate and encourage businesses and residents to reduce emissions through a shift in practices.

- Sustainable Food—These programs and policies are designed to cultivate, support, and provide access to local, sustainably grown agriculture.
- Sustainable City Government—The aim is to develop policies and procedures that encourage sustainability practices throughout the government and its operations.
- Citizen Advisory Committee—The creation of an advisory committee encourages citizen involvement and input into the development of programs and policies throughout the municipality and neighboring counties.
- Green Building—This program is described below.

In January 2009, the Office of Sustainable Development merged with the Bureau of Planning to further encourage larger themes of sustainability and a holistic approach to the movement.

6.4.3 Portland's Green Building Program

Both the city and PDC have green building programs that are closely aligned and work together but have different responsibilities, as described in section 6.4. Both programs offer training and technical assistance to individuals in the development community. While the green building initiative is only a fraction of the scope of the Bureau of Planning and Sustainability, it is unarguably important and a solid program within the community. The Green Building Program has its roots in a multidisciplinary volunteer group that worked with the city council on decisions regarding sustainable development. The Green Building Program was created in 2000; a number of initiatives and products created before then were its precursors.

The Green Building Options Study, undertaken to identify possible policy and programs that would help to establish green building as the go-to standard in the Portland area, aimed to:

- Identify key local green building stakeholders;
- Develop a consensus definition of green building;
- Identify the reasons why green building is important to the city;
- Identify existing regional, state, and local programs that promote green building practices;
- Identify obstacles the city must overcome to help increase green building practices in Portland;
- Identify policy and program options the city can implement to promote green building practices;
- Provide comprehensive public participation throughout the project.

One result of the report was a list of sixty strategies the city of Portland could pursue. This list was then condensed into a list of six recommendations, including a Citywide Green Building Policy and Ordinance; Green Building Development

Guidelines and Rating System; City Facilities Operations and Maintenance Practices; City Budgeting Analysis Process and Financial Tools for Construction and Maintenance Projects; Inter-Bureau Green Building Assistance Program; and Green Building Incentives. These recommendations clearly indicate a dedication within the community and local government to promoting green building strategies and themes.

The Green Building Initiative document that followed focused on two goals: (1) expanding market demand by educating building industry professionals and the public about the benefits of green building; and (2) making green building practices easier to implement by reducing regulatory and financial barriers and developing technical services and resources for building industry professionals.

The overall program includes a number of smaller programs that are valuable to the community and to the furtherance of the green building movement; such as financial incentives, technical services, review of municipal proposals on the table, a green development resource center, residential building resources, case studies, newsletters, research documents, green building strategies, courses, and even a regional green building hotline that offers support over the phone.

6.4.4 Available Guides
Amid all the information, resources, and programs developed and hosted by the Green Building Program, three building guide-

books can be used on, or downloaded from, the Bureau of Planning and Sustainability Web site (www.portlandonline.com/bps).

The *Green Home Remodeling Guide* focuses on residential improvements. The guide caters to a range of budgets and personal inclinations, providing information to homeowners and contractors on a variety of strategies to consider. It contains information on energy and water savings, such as possibilities for incorporating renewable energy in the home, gathering and using rainwater, and protecting nearby streams and waterways from contaminated runoff. It also offers considerable information about local materials and construction methods, durability and maintenance, and how to reduce indoor air pollutants to accomplish better air quality by reducing chemicals and mold. The *Green Home Remodeling Guide* is available as a pdf download from the Web site or for purchase in hard copy at a few locations in Portland.

The second guide, developed and updated by BPS and PDC, is the *Tenant Improvement Guide*, officially titled *Creating a High Performance Workspace*. This guide is intended for use by contractors, designers, and project managers interested in "high performance commercial tenant improvement." During the 1990s, the Portland market experienced a great deal of commercial development as well as office space shifting that gave rise to a substantial amount of interior upfitting and renovation projects. An appreciation for the burgeoning growth trends in the Portland marketplace and elsewhere in the nation during the 1990s, projected out into the early twenty-first century for Portland (and nationally), provided the impetus for the development and release of the guidebook. The book not only suggests strategies and implementation processes that are beneficial to the environment, but also points out that these are cost-effective and efficient—factors that would definitely make every client happy. In addition to emphasizing energy costs and construction methods, the guide also takes softer costs such as reduced liability, employee health, productivity, and operating costs into account. The *Tenant Improvement Guide* is available as a download from the OSD Web site.

The Portland Bureau of Planning and Sustainability also publishes the *Green Affordable Housing Guide*. On the assumption that most affordable housing projects within the city will be managed and/or funded through the city itself, this document identifies typical "green" construction standards and methods as well as methods that stretch some of the boundaries of what is considered typical. The guide provides designers, contractors, and developers with information about construction practices that produce environmentally friendly houses, as well as a directory of local vendors and services that might be helpful to their projects.

The guide presents twelve "Guiding Principles for Green Affordable Housing," which are applicable not only to projects in Portland but also to other similar projects around the country. Among the guideline categories are Design and Site; Energy Conservation; Water Conservation; Conserving Materials and Resources; Enhanced Indoor Air Quality; and Operations and Maintenance. Each strategy within these categories is labeled either Threshold or Voluntary. Threshold strategies are required for all projects supported by the Portland Development Commission, while Voluntary strategies are suggested and possible, but not required. Following an overview of the guidelines, the individual credits are broken down further. Additional information in the form of "why" and "how" for each credit is provided for the Voluntary credits. Threshold credits include "Cost," which provides assistance in planning and budgeting. Some credits also include a "Code" category to familiarize the design team with any requirements set out by the city, other governmental bodies, or other organizations. A directory of local vendors is provided in a Resources and Vendors list at the end of each category as additional support to users of the guide.

6.4.5 Incentives

In addition to the municipal and state tax incentives that are becoming more frequent around the country, Portland's previous OSD created the Green Investment Fund (GIF), a competitive grant program available to public or private projects with industrial, commercial, multi-family residential, or mixed-use programs. Funding has varied year to year: in 2008, funding totaled $425,000. The goal of the program was to emphasize and provide awards to outstanding examples of green building and, secondarily, to help offset the initial costs of new or extensive technologies. The fund was jointly sponsored by a number of the city's departments including the Bureau of Environmental Services, the Water Bureau, and the Energy Trust of Oregon, Inc. Unfortunately, the Green Investment Fund was slated to end in 2009.

The Bureau of Planning and Sustainability also provides a Web page (www.portlandonline.com/bps) covering additional financing and incentives, broken out into Energy-Efficient Mortgages; Financial Incentives for Residential; Financial Incentives for Commercial; and Incentives for Business in Portland. There are other incentive opportunities, including the Energy Trust of Oregon (www.energytrust.org) and the Oregon Business Energy tax credit, hosted by the Oregon Department of Energy. These encourage recycling, energy efficiency, and lower carbon footprints through funding great than one million dollars, essentially paying for the green investments required to achieve LEED Gold certification for buildings of at least 80,000 square feet. Each of these items links to other resources.

6.5 Santa Monica, California

Just to the west of downtown Los Angeles, Santa Monica sits on the beautiful Pacific coastline of California. Justifiably, Santa Monica has made a name for itself through its "commitment to protecting the environment, improving quality of life, and promoting sustainability."

The Santa Monica Green Building Program is an initiative of the city of Santa Monica. At the end of May 2008, the city put a New Green Building Ordinance into effect. The new ordinance takes the existing green building standards and increases the requirements in them, demonstrating the city's dedication to sustainability via this raising of the bar.

6.5.1 Santa Monica's Green Building Program

Santa Monica's green building movement dates back to 1994 when the city council embraced the Santa Monica Sustainable City Program. The program was created by the city's Task Force on the Environment to look more holistically at how Santa Monica could become a truly sustainable city. The goal of the task force was to review the needs of both current and future residents, looking at alternative ways of living that protect and strengthen local natural resources, eliminate harm to both residents and the natural environment, and support the local economy and community. The task force also considered the high cost of some strategies.

Ultimately, the task force recommended the creation and adaptation of Green Building Design and Construction Guidelines generated collaboratively by city staffers and a sustainable-design consultant over a three-year time frame, with

Required Practices	Environment	Ease of Use	Benefits	Capital Cost
MAa - Require Recycling of Demolition & Construction Waste in Construction Contracts	✓✓	✓✓	✓	$
MAb - Specify Recycled Products per EPA purchasing guidelines	✓✓	✓✓✓	✓✓✓	$
Suggested Practices				
MA1 - Restore & Incorporate Portions or Entire Existing Buildings in New Designs	✓✓✓	✓	✓✓✓	$$
MA2 - Specify Reuse of Salvaged Building & Landscape Materials	✓✓✓	✓	✓✓	$
MA3 - Design with Panel, Precut & Engineered Construction Products to Minimize Waste	✓✓	✓✓✓	✓	$

Santa Monica provides a helpful chart outlining their Required/Suggested Practices, with indicators for impact on the environment, ease of use of the strategy, benefits of the strategy, and upfront capital costs. Chart content courtesy of Santa Monica's Green Building Program

considerable contributions by members of the local design and construction industry to ensure that the process and the guidelines were both consensus-driven. This approach encouraged buy-in from the parties affected and thus eased the introduction of the guidelines.

6.5.2 Santa Monica's "Green" Municipal Code Ordinances

Local governments generally choose either to create their own guidelines and requirements for green building to the extent that they are able, or to adopt from elsewhere established guidelines that they feel apply to their community and cover all the necessary bases. In Santa Monica, the guidelines list a number of municipal code ordinances geared toward setting a higher environmental standard for the construction industry.

For example, the Green Building Ordinance, adopted in 2008 in Section 8.108 of the Santa Monica Municipal Code, addresses energy efficiency, green construction materials, landscape water conservation, and construction/demolition waste management. The ordinance sets targets but is not always explicit on how to go about achieving them. Regarding energy efficiency, for example, the ordinance allows the project either to be 10 percent better than code, or to choose from a list of prescriptive measures, such as using ENERGY STAR appliances and a more efficient water heater, as acceptable methods. This process is consistent with the way in which other non-green-related building codes are written.

Other ordinances, however, in Santa Monica and elsewhere, may be seen as more of a finish line than an actual map to get to the end point, setting targets without explaining how to achieve them. For instance, zoning laws state how much parking has to be provided, but not where to put it.

6.5.3 Santa Monica's Green Building Design and Construction Guidelines

The actual Green Building Design and Construction Guidelines include both obligatory and suggested strategies that aim not only to influence the design and construction of future buildings but also to impact the operations and maintenance of the structures. Specifically, the guidelines address commercial and municipal developments in Santa Monica as well as major remodel projects. Instead of stopping with first costs and immediate issues, the guidelines look into life cycle issues and larger environmental impacts than guidelines established earlier in other locations. The guidelines apply to a number of different building types, including Institutional and Commercial Offices, Light Industrial Buildings, Commercial Retail Buildings, Multi-Family Residences, and Hotels and Motels. Notably, single-family housing, high-rises, and heavy industrial buildings are not addressed by these guidelines. The Web site that hosts the guidelines is extremely helpful and well organized, presenting the guideline structure and information in a tool bar. (At the time of writing, the Web site was scheduled for redesign; the description that follows is based on early 2009.) As you click on the "Guidelines" link, the contents roll out in outline form, allowing you to see a number of potential categories of interest.

The Introduction to the guidelines is quite thorough and helpful. It provides basic background information about green design for those who may be interested but are new to the field. Helpful links answer the basic what, why, and how questions of green building through the eyes of Santa Monica, and roll into more tangible and practical information about process, general strategies, and local ordinances as summarized above.

The individual chapters of the guidelines follow the general skeleton of green building and construction issues, addressing eleven different categories to consider during the project. The categories are broken down into a smaller scale than those seen in national guidelines, helping projects to compartmentalize and focus specifically on issues at the local level. The areas addressed are: Siting and Form; Landscape; Transportation; Envelope and Space Planning; Materials; Water Systems; Electrical Systems; HVAC Systems; Control Systems; Construction Management; and Commissioning.

The Introduction also contains a helpful page that addresses how to use the guidelines and reviews the structure of each chapter and what you can expect to find there. The information seems to be tailored to those just entering the green building field, offering potential strategies for consideration without inundating the reader. The primary categories in each chapter include:

- Introduction—Reviews objectives of the chapter and gives an overview of potential credible strategies
- Summary of Required and Recommended Practices—Lists the required sustainable management and design practices as outlined by code, while also providing a table of suggested practices
- Required Practices
- Recommended Practices
- Further Information.

The Summary section includes a useful chart that puts all the required and suggested practices side by side and attempts to compare apples to apples by breaking the strategies down into common categories: Environment, Ease of Use, Other Benefits, and Capital Cost, as seen in the accompanying chart. Between one and three checks are provided for each strategy within each category, allowing for easy visual comparison. The Capital Cost category is measured with one to three dollar signs.

Each of the practices is currently linked to more in-depth pages that provide an overview of the strategy, the intent, and potential cautions regarding the specific tactic. Once you get into the actual chapters, between four (Commissioning) and sixteen (Construction Management) strategies are reviewed and available for consideration. A smaller chart recaps the benefits, as can be seen in the Suggested Practices chart. An additional chart is also provided that identifies related practices with Web links to those pages. For example, in the Materials > Reused Salvaged Materials section, Linked Practices leads to:

- Use existing buildings
- Demolition plan
- Salvage reusable material
- Protect landscape to be retained
- Crush waste concrete
- Further information.

These links and associations are helpful for understanding the synergies between and among strategies, and what methods can help in more than one arena. This is a notion frequently overlooked by those formulating green building guidelines in favor of specific strategies, cost analyses, and quantitative requirements.

Because these are local guidelines, they can also offer additional local information that national guidelines currently cannot provide. For example, Appendix B addresses weather and includes handy charts about local wind speed and direction, heating and cooling degree days in Santa Monica, the average cloud cover, and typical air temperatures. Appendix A does not contain information so locally specific, but it does provide extremely useful information such as a specification for construction waste management, a chart of typical repair and replacement cycles for common building materials, and general checklists for pollution control, life cycle, and resource efficiency. These are all pieces of very useful information, even beyond the city of Santa Monica and southern California.

Santa Monica's Green Building Program also provides a list of case studies of projects in the area that provide valuable insight for those undertaking new local green projects. There is an extensive list of Additional Resources, including local green building suppliers and retailers and links to nonprofits, additional case studies, economic references, design and technology resources, financial incentives, life cycle assessment tools, and more. Santa Monica is definitely encouraging construction projects to "go green" with a local emphasis, but it is also providing sources and reference materials beyond the local level, understanding and embracing steps others have taken and using them to forward the city's movement locally.

6.5.4 Additional Support

Beyond the guidelines and ordinances for commercial and mixed-use just described, there are a number of additional programs and resources that were being emphasized as this book was being written in 2008. First and foremost, additional green building ordinances had been recently updated, increasing the required standards for different categories and criteria.

For example, instead of simply abiding by the checklist without verification, projects now have to submit the checklist when they apply for a permit. Projects are not necessarily checked on all the measures identified in the document, but the idea is that requiring the checklist to be filled out and submitted gets the project team thinking about green design strategies beyond what the city requires. The requirement for building materials increased from four materials with recycled content to five materials selected from a list of Green Materials (see www.smgreen.org for more information).

Another offering is the Green Building Resource Center, managed by Global Green, USA, with help from the city. The center provides a home for material samples, resource lists, local service providers, and staff and serves as a hub of green building information for all concerned. Other offerings on the city's Web site include cost/benefit reports, case study links, and a new Green Affordable Housing checklist developed by Global Green.

6.5.5 Incentives

As mentioned above, Santa Monica has stated that it is aware of the financial burdens that are perceived to accompany sustainable design and has created a number of incentives to help make the process and monetary costs a little easier to take.

One of the common incentives accorded project teams engaging in green design around the country is expedited permitting. The city of Santa Monica has implemented expedited

Global Green USA: *Founded in 1993 by activist and philanthropist Diane Meyer Simon, Global Green (www.global-green.org) is the American arm of Green Cross International (GCI), which was created by former Soviet President Mikhail S. Gorbachev to foster a global value shift toward a sustainable and secure future by reconnecting humanity with the environment. Global Green USA is the only national environmental nonprofit headquartered in southern California that has offices in New Orleans, Washington, DC, and New York, and is one of thirty-one national GCI affiliates throughout the world. The Global Green Resource Center is a partnership of Global Green USA and the city of Santa Monica.*

plan checks for LEED registered projects, potentially taking weeks away from the proposed process. This kind of expediting is being offered not only in southern California but also in other places around the country because the process is a win-win—that is, it is highly beneficial to projects and of little cost consequence to the municipality.

The city of Santa Monica has provided a great deal of valuable information on how to build green within its boundaries and beyond. Not only does it encourage the use of USGBC's LEED, but it also encourages project teams to use rating systems and resources developed by others, such as CHPS for schools, GreenPoint Rated, Green Globes, and Global Green USA.

Although USGBC is the biggest and most well-known creator of green guidelines, the city of Santa Monica is clearly willing to look beyond the most widely used methods. It is encouraging to see Santa Monica providing factual, easily accessible data, such as climate and weather data for design teams to use. Ready access to applicable data simplifies the process and may provide help to project teams that are feeling overwhelmed by their first green building endeavor.

CHPS for schools: *The Collaborative for High Performance Schools (CHPS) (www.chps.net) was created to facilitate the design, construction, and operation of schools that perform exceptionally in both energy and resource efficiency while also creating environments to facilitate quality education. The organization identifies the following criteria as important to high performance school design and construction: healthy; comfortable; energy efficient; material efficient; easy to maintain and operate; commissioned; environmentally responsive site; a building that teaches; safe and secure; community resource; stimulating architecture; and adaptable to changing needs. CHPS has a membership structure accommodating governments, contractors, professional firms, etc., and provides benefits such as trainings, presentations, events, publications, and additional resources material resources and acoustic fact sheets.*

> **GreenPoint Rated:** *GreenPoint Rated is a program of Build It Green (www.builditgreen.org), a nonprofit established in 2003 in Berkeley, CA, to advocate for healthy, energy- and resource-efficient homes in California. In addition to offerings such as government support, collaboration forums, professional training, and consumer education, the organization also offers the GreenPoint Rated program (www.builditgreen.org/greenpoint-rated), which they call a report card for your home. A Certified GreenPoint Rater evaluates the home on the five categories of Energy Efficiency, Resource Conservation, Indoor Air Quality, Water Conservation, and Community, looking in two discrete categories of Existing and New homes.*

6.6 Scottsdale, Arizona

Scottsdale, Arizona, is another national leader in the green building movement at the local level. Scottsdale's sustainability efforts have evolved from a number of environmental planning programs begun in the 1980s and 1990s, including the Environmentally Sensitive Lands Ordinance, Sensitive Design Guidelines, and the McDowell Mountain Preserve.

Scottsdale has used a hybrid approach to create its local guidelines. Drawing on green building systems and programs from other regions and nationally, Scottsdale created or adapted approaches to green building in ways that suit the city's needs.

While the city of Scottsdale's Green Building Program was launched in early 1998, the foundation for the program started nearly three years earlier when the city's Building Official collaborated with members of the residential construction community to develop a green building program. Between volunteers and the staff of the city's building department, a committee researched similar programs around the country and gathered perinent information for their own development of green building guidelines. A formal committee called the Green Building Advisory Committee (GBAC) was created in 1998 by the city's Environmental Quality Advisory Board, and was responsible for overseeing the development of Scottsdale's residential green building program. The program is now administered out of the newly created Office of Environmental Initiatives division.

6.6.1 Scottsdale's Green Building Construction Guidelines

Part of the green building program's success stems from its full integration with the building plan review department, allowing for streamlined review, incentives, standardization, and better customer service. Within this framework, Scottsdale has established a number of other green building rating checklists:

Residential (1998); Commercial (2001); Tenant Improvements (2001); and Multi-Family (2007).

Residential

Focusing locally on the climate of the Sonoran Desert and trends in construction, the Scottsdale team decided that the creation of a residential green building program was most pressing. After reviewing both established and budding residential programs around the country, the team decided on a voluntary, non-regulatory, free program not requiring any type of organization membership. Scottsdale's first Residential Green Building Checklist was developed to rate residences in the standard green building environmental impact categories: site, energy, building materials, indoor air quality, water, and solid waste. As is typical of rating systems, a minimum number of points out of the 150 items on the checklist was required. A 2006 revision of the checklist jumped the points required to a minimum of 50 points for Entry Level and 100 points to achieve an Advanced Level. Special Options created opportunities to receive bonus points. The fourteen rating categories remained unchanged:

- Site
- Structural Elements
- Energy Rating/Performance
- Thermal Envelope
- Heating, Ventilation, and Air Conditioning
- Electrical Power, Lighting, Appliances
- Plumbing System
- Roofing
- Exterior Finishes
- Interior Finishes
- Interior Doors, Cabinetry, Trim
- Flooring
- Solid Waste
- Innovative Design

There are twenty-eight prerequisites. These are devoid of points and range across the board in topic. Each is paired with a statement about why the measure is important, transporting the checklist from simply a prescriptive element into a truly educational tool. For example, item 21 from the checklist reads:

Design and install individually switched task lighting in at least 3 separate task areas (e.g., bathroom vanity, kitchen counter, laundry). *Built-in task lighting provides specific use lighting in lieu of general purpose lighting, lowering the amount of energy used in the home.* (Italics added)

After the prerequisites, the checklist provides a more standard version of credits, requirements, and options, organized by category. Each credit is accompanied by a statement that explains the underlying reasoning and purpose to help bring up the knowledge level of each individual that reads through the document.

Commercial

Scottsdale's Commercial Green Building checklist was influenced by a number of other established commercial guidelines such as LEED, Austin Energy's Commercial Program, and BREEAM. The version current at this writing has four rating levels: Level 1 meets all prerequisites; Level 2 achieves 25 percent–49 percent of checklist items; Level 3 achieves 50 percent–74 percent of checklist items; and Level 4 achieves 75 percent or more of checklist items. The categories mirror the LEED rating system but use credits refined to fit the local climate and bioregion. Scottsdale's program also incorporates more prescriptive measures for both prerequisites and rating options.

Unlike the Residential checklist, the commercial version does not include extra information for educational purposes. It is, instead, a highly condensed and structured document.

Multi-Family

The Multi-Family checklist is very similar to the Residential checklist. While the primary structure is the same, and many credits are almost duplicated word-for-word, occasional credits are added, adapted, or eliminated based on the fact that single-family homes and multi-family homes are two different creatures. For example, the residential credit HVAC 5.6—"Install a 'whole house' fan to ventilate the house with outside air during seasonal transition months (spring, early summer, autumn)"— is eliminated from the Multi-Family checklist. These types of credits may not make as much sense in a larger project due to the complexity of installation in stacked units. The Multi-Family checklist recognizes the inherent resource efficiencies of clustered and high-density residential developments, such as the added insulation from shared partitions between units.

Commercial Tenant Improvement

In the same way that the Multi-Family checklist is a close sibling to the Residential checklist, the Commercial Tenant Improvement checklist is a close relative to the Commercial checklist. With the same categories and same four levels of achievement, the Tenant Improvement checklist has been revised and truncated somewhat to appeal to shell upfits. As in other tenant build-out checklists, Scottsdale's Tenant Improvement checklist speaks to topics such as building selection for future offices and green elements of the chosen building.

The checklist also considers how a building is operated with respect to tenant space and lease negotiations, emphasizing how tenant demand may help create a shift in the marketplace. While some lease negotiations help an individual company understand their impact and resource use (such as the ability to sub-meter and see their specific contribution to energy consumption), other leasing options suggest that other companies may be interested in different facility standards illustrating a greater dedication to the environment (such as onsite renewable systems). Because real estate is a consumer-driven world, tenants have some power through their demands and requirements for leases regarding what types of spaces are being made available. This power is being identified in a number of tenant improvement guidelines and is certainly seen in Scottsdale.

6.6.2 Additional Publications

Like many other local programs, Scottsdale offers more than just guidelines. Some of these other offerings will be covered in the following Incentive section; others are publications the city makes available. The *Green Home Buyers Guide* is a pamphlet with a mini-checklist to help home buyers understand what to look for when searching for a "green" home. This type of document speaks directly to those who are not in the design and construction industry, translating industry terms and concepts into more easily understood words. The pamphlet addresses such issues as "The Right Site and Location" and "The Right Design," broken down into specific qualifiers for each topic. For instance, "The Right Site and Location" considers: farmers' markets located in the area; shade trees planted on the east and west sides of the house; and making a neighborhood conducive for walking and biking.

"The Right Exterior" addresses the: minimum use of skylights to reduce heat gain (suggesting light tubes instead); using reusable/recyclable roofing materials such as metal or concrete; and evenly distributed attic insulation of at least R-30. These are issues that could be answered easily by a home inspector or possibly a realtor, if not by home buyers themselves.

Another valuable publication from Scottsdale is *Green Building: Home Remodeling Guidelines*, which looks at the different possibilities for remodeling a home, particularly one in Scottsdale, from the standpoints of: Site Use and Landscaping, Energy Performance, Indoor Environmental Quality, Kitchen Remodel, Bathroom Remodel, Additions and Enclosures, and Room Improvements. Each of these chapters contains an overview, suggested guidelines, and design considerations, and covers specific issues such as appliances, flooring, and cabinetry (the Kitchen Remodel section), and occupant activity control and building maintenance (the Indoor Environmental Quality section).

Information is about integrated design and construction waste management; universal design, and life cycle cost are also addressed. While these terms are becoming fairly prevalent in the construction industry, they are still rarely heard in the non-construction world of home ownership. The coverage reflects Scottsdale's efforts to go beyond mere regulation and suggested guidelines by demonstrating dedication to educating people about green building.

Also available on Scottsdale's green building Web site is

the *Residential Landscape Revitalization Workbook*, a document similar to *Home Remodeling Guidelines.* It lays out the process of redefining outdoor residential space, starting with conceptual design and considerations, from Before Beginning Your Project to Identifying Existing Conditions, Choose a Design Theme, Put it All Together, and Implement the Landscape Plan. Resources galore follow these primary topics. In addition to providing step-by-step instructions on creating a beautiful landscape, the publication emphasizes creating a local landscape that lives lightly on the land without overstressing the resources provided, explains microclimates and cautions against potentially (even inadvertently) altering them, and addresses "free water" or rainwater and runoff. It also takes into account orientation and structural considerations (where windows are located in the home and how the landscape can benefit them.

6.6.3 Incentives

As a community- and consumer-driven program, Scottsdale's Green Building Program originally had little funding from the city itself. The program established a number of incentives to encourage involvement. Once the Green Building Program became housed under the Building Department, the most obvious tactic was to reduce the plan review time for qualified green building projects. In Scottsdale, the time for permit review is cut by up to one-third, depending on the complexity of the project.

Another key motivation for the community to get involved in green building programs is the promise of education. Guided by the categories found in the checklist, the city of Scottsdale offers tours, seminars, workshops, expositions, and lectures. Spring 2009 marks the eleventh Annual Green Building Expo. A free Green Building lecture series is a monthly event, presenting a range of topics from manufactured wall and roof systems to green feng shui. For builders and owners interested in green building, additional incentives include signs for the job site, a directory of green-friendly builders and designers, homeowners' manuals, and promotional and marketing packages for builders and developers.

In the area of monetary incentives, Arizona provides tax credits for installing a residential greywater conservation system. The benefit for individual homeowners is currently 25 percent of the system and installation, not to exceed $1,000; As of 2008 the credit was $200 per home if a developer or corporation is building the residence and neighborhood.

The state also offers a number of financial and tax incentives for solar energy through energy suppliers, to capitalize on the plentiful sun in the desert. Depending on the energy service provider, there are rebates and tax incentives for both photovoltaic and solar thermal water heating systems.

6.7 Wisconsin

Green building guidelines in Madison, Wisconsin, focus on residential applications. Like Arlington, Virginia, Madison draws heavily on well-established national guidelines to address commercial construction and to create local guidelines for the res-idential market. While Madison itself does not have a centralized online source of green building information, the Wisconsin Green Building Alliance (www.wgba.org) may be useful to those in the city and, for that matter, throughout the state who want to build green.

The guidelines Madison has created and adopted are based on LEED but without the obligation to pursue actual registration and certification. (The Green Built Home Program, which focuses on Madison's residential market, is described in section 6.7.4.) Before presenting that discussion, however, a look at what's happening at the state policy level is relevant to commercial, institutional, and residential builders.

6.7.1 State Policy Overview

The state of Wisconsin has developed a solid collection of policies encouraging the development of sustainable buildings. Anyone building anywhere in Wisconsin should become familiar with its requirements. The following information is based on a draft report completed for the state of Wisconsin's Office of Energy Independence in the fall of 2007 by Joshua Clements; and it covers the key areas of interest for green builders.

Energy

A number of the energy-related criteria being applied in Wisconsin are specific to state facilities and have been set forth in various state acts and executive orders. For example, Wisconsin Act 141, signed into law in 2006, focuses on the state's renewable energy portfolio. The goal of the act is to increase the state's portfolio standard to a total of 10 percent renewable energy by 2015. To accomplish this, Act 141 requires that state facilities be purchasing 10 percent of their needed annual energy from renewable sources by the end of calendar year 2006 and 20 percent by the end of 2011.

Wisconsin Executive Order 145, signed in 2006, stipulates that state facilities should be 30 percent more energy efficient than the standard commercial code. Additional energy reduction goals mandate at least a 10 percent reduction by 2008 and 20 percent by 2010. An Energy-Use Policy established in 2006 recognizes that building design is not the only factor that is important to energy efficiency. Two other factors are at least equally important: the phases of inhabiting and using the building, and the way in which the building is managed, operated, and maintained. The policy includes the development and dissemination to operations personnel of management strategies and preferred tactics for reducing energy consumption, including maintenance issues, in state facilities to operations personnel. The strategies include thermostat settings, lighting, workshop equipment, finishes, building automation, and water conservation.

An Energy Design Guideline for the state, established in 2007, focuses on reducing the use of fossil fuels within state-owned facilities. Along with other directives, such as *Incorporate environmentally responsible and sustainable concepts and practices into the planning, design and construction, as described in the state's sustainable design guidelines,* the guidelines focus on attaining the highest energy efficiency and the lowest energy consumption possible. The mandate also incorporates the idea of life cycle costing and passive strategies and emphasizes the value of an integrated design approach within projects.

Life Cycle Costing

Life cycle costing refers to the understanding and incorporation of whole-life elements—such as maintenance, operation, repair, employee health, etc.—into the appraisal of the project. Often, when discussing the creation of a new building or major renovation, the only financial costs considered are the upfront costs, such as material and construction costs. Maintenance staff (if they are consulted) may pay attention to cleaning and repair, but frequently these and other more distant costs are overlooked for more immediate expenses.

Earlier I noted that a number of the national green building guideline systems have either not yet incorporated the idea of life cycle analysis and cost into their structures or are just in the process of doing so. Wisconsin, on the other hand, created specific guidelines for life cycle costing in state building projects as early as 1994 following the issuance of a general policy on the subject.

The General Policy on Life Cycle Costing (LCC) states, "Life cycle costing is an economic evaluation used to compare alternatives. The procedure for use on state building projects shall consider all relevant cost associated with each building alternative during its life cycle, discount them to a common point in time, and provide a comparison to determine the alternative with the lowest total life cycle cost." The life cycle costing process is very complex—both detailed and layered—which is why many entities creating guidelines are struggling with how to incorporate the concept. Wisconsin's approach has been to include the following:

- Life span
- Initial cost of building systems and components
- Criteria such as maintenance, energy use, staffing, transportation, and other operating costs for alternative options
- A rate reflecting the "earning power of money and purchasing power due to inflation"
- A bond rate expressing bonds sold by the state (tax supported to help sustain the state's building program.)

Similarly, by setting out to understand and incorporate life cycle costing in state guidelines, Wisconsin discovered that there are a number of obstacles to the inclusion of this approach. State guidelines identify four: the Wisconsin Building Code itself; physical restrictions incorporated in the project (such as site, utility sourcing, adjacencies, etc.); program-defined requirements and function; and the frequently blamed budget.

Daylighting

Wisconsin has one other free standing green standard in place, concerning daylighting in state facilities. This guide, created in 2003, outlines general criteria for addressing natural daylighting and its benefits in state-owned buildings. Some of the criteria included in the guide are that it:

- Fosters occupant comfort and health, while increasing individual enjoyment and efficiency;
- Includes both increased environmentally responsible design and construction practices in projects; and
- Decreases a project's peak electricity requirements.

Additional criteria in the guide are similarly imprecise, but examples of design standards are also given to help project teams achieve or exceed the stated daylighting goals. These elements include glass performance, reflectance factors of interior finishes, ceiling heights, and exterior solar shading devices. As is true in many other places, Wisconsin's guidelines give design teams direction and goals without a specific roadmap.

6.7.2 Wisconsin Environmental Initiative Overview

Created in 1995, the Wisconsin Environmental Initiative (WEI) was modeled on a highly successful program in Minnesota, the structure and intent of which was similar to what Wisconsin was seeking. The Minnesota Environmental Initiative (MEI), launched four years earlier, was established to educate and facilitate environmental solutions, not necessarily to lobby for policy change. Similarly, WEI was created as a neutral nonprofit focused on education. The goal of WEI is to allow discussion from all sides, fostering conversation, relationships, and understanding through the organization's events and initiatives. Consult the WEI Web site for more information: www.wi-ei.org.

6.7.3 Green Built Home Program

Green Built Home is a program of the Wisconsin Environmental Initiative and is NAHB-affiliated. In light of this partnership, the program offers a co-branded Home Certification under which national certification and a NAHB/GBH certificate can be granted. Green Built Home won the National Association of Home Builders' 2006 National Program of the Year Award for excellence in the field of residential green building guidelines. Implemented by the Wisconsin Environmental Initiative in partnership with the Madison Area Builders Association, the program evaluates and certifies new and remodeled homes for compliance with sustainable design and energy conservation standards. The number of certified Green Built Homes has been growing dramatically since 1999, when the program was established. In 1999, 30 homes were certified; by 2005 that number had increased to 681; and by 2007 there were 856 certified homes. Totals are still being tallied for 2008 while this is being written.

The first thing an interested builder should consider doing is to enroll in the Green Built Home (GBH) Program. While enrollment is not mandatory to take a project through the review and certification process, GBH uses enrollment to confer membership in the program, giving members a discount on the fee for enrolling a project in the certification program. Details are given on the GBH Web site. The membership enrollment form is simple, consisting of basic contact information, estimated number of projects for the year, and a signature space signalling agreement to allow GBH to use the home and builder for promotional purposes.

Once the builder has enrolled in the GBH program for a new home or remodel to be reviewed and certified, a number of targets must be met. First, the home has to be signed up for the program; this can happen after the start of construction and involves a fee (as mentioned previously). In addition, as of November 1, 2008, new construction homes are required to abide by Wisconsin ENERGY STAR® Homes Certification as well. Remodel projects interested in GBH certification are required to have a preliminary Home Performance with ENERGY STAR energy evaluation. The program requires a completed Green Built Home checklist (described below) and building plans and associated drawings. The plans allow the reviewers to verify the information and design intent as stated on the checklist. Finally, the program requires that, during the construction process, the builder perform calculations to determine the HVAC equipment load and target energy use. Additional required documentation covers project registration, the statement of design intent, the sustainable design strategies being used, and the energy-use reduction goal.

While the bulk of the work for registration can be accomplished while the project is under construction, a few steps need to be completed after the home is finished. These steps entail energy primarily use verification and testing. Third-party verification is required for all home types—new, remodel, and multifamily.

Checklist—Basic Requirements and Categories

In scope and format, the Green Built Home New Home Checklist is similar to other checklists described in this book. Each registered home must meet all eight of the Basic Requirements in Section A of the form as well as earn a minimum of 60 points. These points can be achieved by earning at least the minimum point requirements in Sections B, C, D, and E, plus additional points either from those sections or from any combination of items from the remaining Checklist sections.

The first Basic Requirement pertains to Wisconsin's ENERGY STAR Home standards, including air infiltration testing, ventilation equipment, and fireplace safety. For homes that do not rely on conventional mechanical heating and cooling strategies, alternatives to the Wisconsin ENERGY STAR Home standards are considered on a case-by-case basis. The seven remaining Basic Requirements are: ENERGY STAR Appliances; Erosion Control; Recycling; Use of Tropical Hardwoods; Homeowner Handbook; Certification Plaque and Green Guide Label (for window); and Mercury Thermostats.

Nine categories of credits follow the Basic Requirements. These categories should look very familiar to you:

- Siting and Land Use
- Landscape Conservation and Stormwater Management
- Energy Efficiency (Site Design; Insulation and Air Sealing; Glazing; Mechanical Systems; Appliances; Lighting and Electrical Systems; and Integrated Climatic Design)
- Materials Selection (Below Grade; Structural Frame; Envelope, Walls, and Ceiling; Insulation; Roof; Sub-floor; Finish Floor; Doors, Cabinetry, and Trim)
- Indoor Air Quality (IAQ Materials, IAQ Finishes, and Adhesives)
- Plumbing and Water Conservation (Water Heating)
- Waste Reduction, Recycling, and Disposal
- Builder Operations
- Efficient Use of Space

After checking the boxes and tallying the allotted points in each section, the credits are totaled and the builder signs on the dotted line, certifying that the information is complete and accurate and that all requirements for Green Built Home certification have been met.

Checklist—Point Scale and Certification
The Green Built Home New Home Checklist can be found at http://www.wi-ei.org/uploads/media/GBH_CHKLST_08.pdf. As always, since by the time you read this, an updated version may have supplanted this one, it's always wise to check the Web site. The discussion that follows, however, is based on the 2008 version. As with other systems reviewed, minimum point thresholds have been established for each of the categories:

- Landscape Conservation and Stormwater Management (3 points)
- Energy Efficiency (10 points)
- Materials Selection (6 points)
- Indoor Air Quality (5 points)
- Waste Reduction and Recycling (1 point)

The checklist for Wisconsin's Green Built Home Program is much like those used elsewhere around the country. One notable perk with this system that is not regularly seen in other programs is that once a builder is established as a GBH member in good standing by demonstrating ongoing compliance with GBH standards and submittal requirements, the builder has the option to submit a "baseline" Green Built Specifications checklist that qualifies all homes the builder constructs for GBH certification. Not only does this opportunity allow a builder to certify all of its homes through the GBH program with less paperwork and legwork, it provides a potentially large incentive for home builders to embrace the green building movement. Similar incentives exist for consistency regarding energy efficiency checks and testing.

The same can also be said for state incentives, policies, and codes. The overview of Wisconsin's accomplishments (and the relatively short time frame in which these have occurred) can provide a basis for researching state and local government incentives in other parts of the country. Regardless of where in the country you may be working, and in what capacity with respect to green building, it is helpful to know what various government entities are doing to set the green bar for private enterprise and to encourage builders to engage in green building practices.

Bibliography

Austin Energy. Austin Energy Homepage. Austin Energy, www.austinenergy.com.

Castle, Duke, Logan Cravens, Patrick Driscoll, John Echlin, Paul Schwer, Alan Scott, Charles Stephens, and Dennis Wilde. 2004. "Using the Natural Step as a Framework toward the Construction and Operation of Fully Sustainable Buildings." Edited by The Natural Step, Portland, OR: Oregon Natural Step Construction Industry Group.

City of Arlington. 2003. "Arlington Green Home Choice." Arlington, VA: City of Arlington.

City of Arlington. Environmental Services. Green Building Incentive Program. City of Arlington, www.arlingtonva.us/departments/EnvironentalServices/epo/EnvironmentalServicesEpoIncentiveProgram.aspx.

City of Santa Monica. Santa Monica Green Building Program. City of Santa Monica, www.smgreen.org.

City of Scottsdale. Green Building Program. SCOTTSDALEAZ.GOV: The Official Web Site of the City of Scottsdale, Arizona, www.scottsdaleaz.gov/greenbuilding.

City of Scottsdale. 2004. Scottsdale Green Building Program Progress Report. Scottsdale, AZ: City of Scottsdale.

City of Scottsdale. 2006. Scottsdale Green Building Progress Report 2005. Scottsdale, AZ: City of Scottsdale.

Friedrichs, Gillian, Shannon Tocchini, Sue Bartlett, and Jaime Sanz de Santamaria, eds. 2003. *The Eco-Indicators: Findings from the TNS Eco-Indicators Peer Learning Group.* Portland, OR: Oregon Natural Step Network.

GBI. Green Building Initiative Homepage. GBI, www.thegbi.org.

NAHB. 2006. NAHB Model Green Home Building Guidelines, Washington, DC: NAHB.

NAHB. National Association of Homebuilders Homepage. NAHB, www.nahb.org.

North Carolina HealthyBuilt Homes. Healthy Built Homes Program. North Carolina Solar Center, www.healthybuilthomes.org.

Roberts, Lin. 2007. A Systems Framework for Sustainability and Its Application to a Construction Project. Paper presented at International Conference on Sustainability Engineering and Science, February 20–23, in Auckland, New Zealand.

Thomas, J. Matthew. 2006. Code Green—Santa Fe, New Mexico. Santa Fe, New Mexico: The City of Santa Fe.

TNS. The Natural Step Homepage. The Natural Step. www.thenaturalstep.org.

USGBC. 2005. LEED-NC: Green Building Rating System for New Construction & Major Renovations, Version 2.2. Washington, DC: USGBC.

USGBC. U.S. Green Building Council Home Page. USGBC, www.usgbc.org.

WEI. 2008. "Green Built Home New Home Checklist." Madison, WI: Wisconsin Environmental Initiative.

Wisconsin Environmental Initiative. Green Built Home. Wisconsin Environmental Initiative. www.greenbuilthome.org.

Index